Creating Safe Spaces

How to Build Comfort Zones in Your Life for Anxiety Management

Michelle Mann

Copyright © 2024 by Michelle Mann

All rights reserved.

No portion of this book may be reproduced in any form without written permission from the publisher or author, except as permitted by U.S. copyright law.

Contents

1. Introduction   1
2. The Nature of Anxiety   11
3. Anxiety Disorders   19
4. Recognizing Your Anxiety Triggers   33
5. Crafting Your Personal Safe Space   59
6. Safc Spaces at Home   80
7. Establishing Boundaries for a Safe Work Environment   96
8. Social Interactions and Anxiety   119
9. Creating Mental and Emotional Safe Zones   145
10. Maintaining Your Safe Space Over Time   163
11. Conclusion   179
12. Appendix 1   182
13. Worksheet 1   185

14.	Worksheet 2	189
15.	Worksheet 3	192
16.	Worksheet 4	195
17.	Worksheet 5	197
18.	Appendix 2	198
19.	Acknowledgments	204

Introduction

"The best way out is always through."

- Robert Frost

In our whirlwind of a world, where chaos often reigns and moments of tranquility seem few and far between, discovering places where we can truly breathe easy can feel like stumbling upon buried treasure. But nestled within the notion of safe spaces lies something truly transformative—a chance not only to reshape the places we inhabit but also to reshape how we navigate life itself. So, welcome aboard our journey into the heart of "The Power of Safe Spaces." Here, we'll dive deep into the remarkable influence these sanctuaries of solace and empathy wield over our happiness and development.

The Power of Safe Spaces

In our increasingly interconnected yet often isolating world, the concept of safe spaces holds profound significance. Beyond mere physical confines, safe spaces serve as emotional sanctuaries where individuals can shed the masks they wear and reveal their true selves. Within these havens of acceptance and understanding, the rigid barriers that often separate us from one another dissolve, paving the way for authentic connection and mutual support.

At the heart of safe spaces lies a deep sense of validation and respect. Here, individuals are not judged for their flaws or shortcomings but celebrated for their inherent worth and unique perspectives. Whether it's a cozy corner of a bustling café, a virtual gathering space in the digital realm, or the comforting presence of a trusted friend, safe spaces offer solace and refuge from the pressures of daily life.

In these nurturing environments, vulnerability is not seen as a weakness but as a courageous act of self-expression. Walls come down, masks are discarded, and individuals are free to share their joys, sorrows, hopes, and fears without fear of ridicule or rejection. It is within these moments of raw authenticity that true connections are forged, transcending superficiality, and fostering deep bonds of empathy and understanding.

Moreover, safe spaces serve as incubators for personal growth and empowerment. In an atmosphere of acceptance and support, individuals are encouraged to explore their passions, pursue their dreams, and confront their fears with newfound courage and resilience. Whether it's overcoming past traumas, challenging societal norms, or daring to pursue unconventional paths, safe spaces provide the fertile ground upon which individuals can cultivate their fullest potential.

Ultimately, the power of safe spaces lies in their ability to nourish the human spirit and foster a sense of belonging and connection in an often-fragmented world. They remind us that, despite our differences, we are all deserving of love, respect, and understanding. As we journey through life's ups and downs, let us cherish and cultivate these sacred spaces wherever we find them, knowing that within their embrace, we are truly home.

Finding My Safe Space

When I was a child and teen, I always felt like I was walking on a tightrope, trying to balance the expectations of others with my own desires and dreams. As a shy and introverted teenager, navigating the complexities of high school social dynamics felt like an insurmountable challenge. I longed for a place where I could escape the judgmental eyes of my peers and simply be myself—a refuge from the relentless pressure to fit in and conform.

It wasn't until I stumbled upon the school's drama club that I found my safe haven. Tucked away in a forgotten corner of the campus, the drama club room was a sanctuary of creativity and acceptance—a world where differences were celebrated, and quirks were cherished.

Stepping into that dimly lit room for the first time felt like coming home. Surrounded by kindred spirits who shared my love for storytelling and self-expression, I felt a sense of belonging that I had never experienced before. Here, amidst the chaos of rehearsals and the laughter of fellow cast members, I discovered the transformative power of safe spaces.

In the confines of the drama club room, I shed my insecurities and embraced my true self. Whether I was belting out show tunes at the top of my lungs or reciting lines from Shakespeare with gusto, I felt liberated from the weight of societal expectations. The judgmental whispers of my classmates faded into the background, replaced by the supportive cheers of my newfound friends.

As the years passed, the drama club became more than just a extracurricular activity; it became my lifeline—a beacon of light in the darkest of times. Through the ups and downs of adolescence, the drama club provided a refuge where I could escape the chaos of the outside world and find solace in the company of kindred spirits.

Looking back, I realize that the drama club taught me a valuable lesson: that safe spaces are not defined by their physical surroundings, but by the sense of acceptance and belonging they cultivate. In the drama club room, I found the courage to embrace my authentic self and pursue my passions without fear of judgment or rejection.

Today, as I navigate the complexities of adult life, I carry the lessons I learned from the drama club with me wherever I go. Though I may no longer perform on stage, I continue to seek out safe spaces—places where I can connect with others on a deeper level, free from the constraints of societal norms and expectations.

For me, the drama club will always be more than just a memory; it will be a testament to the transformative power of safe spaces—a reminder that, no matter how turbulent life may be, there will always be places where we can find solace, acceptance, and belonging.

How to Use this Book

Navigating "The Power of Safe Spaces" is designed to be as intuitive and empowering as the safe spaces it explores.

Here's how to make the most out of this journey:

Engage with Intention

As you embark on this exploration, approach each chapter with an open mind and a willingness to reflect on your own experiences. Consider keeping a journal to jot down insights, reflections, and action steps that resonate with you.

Explore at Your Own Pace

This book is your personal guide, so feel free to navigate it in a way that suits your needs and preferences. Whether you choose to read it cover to cover or jump to specific chapters that pique your interest, trust your intuition and follow your own unique path.

Reflect and Apply

Throughout the book, you'll encounter thought-provoking questions, exercises, and practical strategies designed to help you deepen your understanding of safe spaces and apply these insights to your own life. Take the time to pause, reflect, and engage with these prompts to unlock your inner wisdom and foster personal growth.

Embrace Vulnerability

The journey toward creating and embracing safe spaces can be both exhilarating and challenging. Be gentle with yourself as you explore your vulnerabilities, confront your fears, and cultivate authentic connections with others. Remember that vulnerability is not a sign of weakness but a catalyst for growth and transformation.

Connect with Others

While this book is a valuable resource in itself, the true power of safe spaces lies in the connections we forge with others. Consider joining a book club, discussion group, or online community where you can share your insights, experiences, and support with like-minded individuals on a similar journey.

Practice Self-Compassion

As you navigate the ups and downs of creating safe spaces in your life, remember to practice self-compassion and kindness toward yourself. Celebrate your successes, acknowledge your challenges, and embrace the messy and imperfect journey of personal growth with grace and humility.

Take Action

The ultimate goal of this book is to empower you to create and nurture safe spaces in your own life. As you gain insights and inspiration from its pages, take proactive steps to incorporate these principles into your daily life. Whether it's setting boundaries, reaching out to supportive individuals, or cultivating self-care practices, every small action brings you one step closer to creating a life filled with safety, connection, and authenticity.

By approaching this book with curiosity, courage, and an open heart, you have the power to transform not only your immediate surroundings but also your entire approach to life. So, dive in, embrace the journey, and let the power of safe spaces guide you toward a life of fulfillment, connection, and joy.

Words of Encouragement

To my fellow travelers on the journey of discovering the power of safe spaces,

As you embark on this exploration of creating spaces of comfort, understanding, and authenticity in your life, I want to offer you words of encouragement and support.

First and foremost, I want you to know that you are not alone. The path towards cultivating safe spaces can sometimes feel daunting or uncertain but remember that countless others are walking alongside you, each with their own unique experiences and challenges. Together, we can uplift and support one another on this journey.

I encourage you to approach this book with an open heart and an open mind. Allow yourself to be vulnerable, to explore your innermost thoughts and feelings, and to embrace the process of self-discovery and growth. Know that it's okay to take things one step at a time, to pause and reflect when needed, and to honor your own pace and journey.

As you delve into the chapters ahead, I invite you to lean into your own resilience and courage. Trust in your ability to navigate challenges, to overcome obstacles, and to emerge stronger and more resilient on the other side. Remember that the moments of discomfort or uncertainty you may encounter are often the very moments where growth and transformation occur.

Above all, I want to remind you to be gentle with yourself. Creating safe spaces in your life is a journey, not a destination, and it's okay to stumble along the way. Offer yourself the same kindness and compassion that you extend to others, and remember that each step forward, no matter how small, is a victory worth celebrating.

You are capable, you are worthy, and you are deserving of the safety, connection, and authenticity that safe spaces offer. Trust in your own inherent strength and resilience and know that you have the power to create a life filled with love, acceptance, and joy.

I believe in you, and I'm cheering you on every step of the way.

The Nature of Anxiety

"Anxiety does not empty tomorrow of its sorrows, but only empties today of its strength."

- *Charles Spurgeon*

Welcome to the first chapter of our journey into the intricate labyrinth of anxiety. As we embark on this journey, our goal is to unravel the multifaceted layers of anxiety, from its fundamental definitions to its profound impact on both our minds and bodies, as well as its pervasive presence in the modern landscape. It is within these depths that we seek not only to comprehend the nature of anxiety but also to unearth pathways toward healing and fortitude.

In this chapter, we will embark on a comprehensive exploration of anxiety, illuminating its essence and implications from various angles. Through careful examination, we will dissect the intricate web of thoughts, emotions, and physiological responses that constitute anxiety, shedding light on its complexity and significance in our lives.

By exploring the foundations of anxiety, we equip ourselves with the tools necessary to navigate its labyrinthine passages. With understanding comes empowerment—the ability to recognize the signs and symptoms of anxiety, to discern its impact on our physiology, and to confront its challenges with resilience and grace.

Moreover, by contextualizing anxiety within the framework of modern society, we gain insight into its prevalence and implications in our daily lives. From the relentless pressures of work and academic expectations to the omnipresence of technology and social media, we uncover the myriad factors that contribute to the proliferation of anxiety in our contemporary world.

Ultimately, our exploration of anxiety serves as a beacon of hope—a guiding light illuminating the path toward healing and resilience. By unraveling the mysteries of anxiety, we pave the way for transformation, empowerment, and growth. Together, let us embark on this journey with open hearts and curious minds, embracing the challenges and opportunities that lie ahead.

Understanding Anxiety

Anxiety is a natural human emotion characterized by feelings of worry, nervousness, or unease about future events or outcomes. It's a common response to stressful or uncertain situations and can vary widely in intensity and duration. While occasional anxiety is normal and even helpful as it can motivate us to prepare for challenges, excessive or persistent anxiety can interfere with daily life and may indicate the presence of an anxiety disorder.

What is the Difference Between Normal Stress & Anxiety?

Understanding the difference between normal stress and anxiety is crucial for recognizing when our responses to challenging situations are within a typical range and when they may indicate a more significant issue. Here's a breakdown of the key distinctions:

Normal Stress

Response to Specific Situations

Stress is a natural response to specific situations or events that are perceived as challenging, demanding, or threatening. It's a normal part of life and can be triggered by various factors such as work deadlines, academic exams, or interpersonal conflicts.

Temporary

Stress is typically temporary and tends to subside once the stressor is removed or the situation is resolved. For example, the stress associated with preparing for a job interview may dissipate once the interview is over.

Motivational

In moderate amounts, stress can be motivational and help individuals focus their attention and energy on addressing the task at hand. It can enhance performance and productivity by sharpening focus and increasing alertness.

Physical Symptoms

Physical symptoms of stress may include increased heart rate, sweating, muscle tension, and shallow breathing. These responses are part of the body's natural stress response system and are typically transient.

Anxiety (*Generalized Worry*)

Anxiety involves persistent, excessive worry or apprehension about future events, situations, or outcomes, often without a specific trigger. It's a pervasive sense of unease that can impact various aspects of life.

Chronic

Unlike stress, which is typically short-lived, anxiety may persist over an extended period, even in the absence of immediate stressors. It can become a chronic condition that affects daily functioning and quality of life.

Disproportionate Response

Individuals with anxiety may experience a disproportionate level of distress or impairment in response to situations that others may perceive as relatively minor or manageable. The intensity of anxiety may not match the severity of the stressor.

Interference with Functioning

Anxiety can interfere with various aspects of life, including work, relationships, and social activities. It may lead to avoidance behaviors, difficulty concentrating, irritability, and disruptions in sleep patterns.

Physical and Psychological Symptoms

In addition to physical symptoms similar to those of stress, such as increased heart rate and muscle tension, anxiety may also manifest with psychological symptoms such as racing thoughts, restlessness, difficulty relaxing, and intrusive worries.

While stress and anxiety share similarities in terms of their physiological responses, duration, and impact on well-being, the key distinction lies in the nature of the response and its persistence over time. While stress is a normal and often adaptive response to specific stressors, anxiety involves persistent, excessive worry and apprehension that can significantly impair functioning and quality of life. Recognizing the difference between normal stress and anxiety can help individuals seek appropriate support and interventions when needed.

Physiological Impact of Anxiety

Anxiety triggers a cascade of physiological responses within the body, collectively known as the stress response or "fight or flight" response. When we perceive a threat, whether real or imagined, our bodies activate this response to prepare us to confront or flee from danger. Some of the key physiological effects of anxiety include:

Increased Heart Rate

Anxiety stimulates the sympathetic nervous system, leading to an accelerated heart rate. This helps pump oxygen-rich blood to essential organs and muscles, preparing the body for action.

Shallow or Rapid Breathing

Anxiety can cause changes in breathing patterns, such as shallow or rapid breathing (hyperventilation). This can lead to symptoms such as dizziness, light-headedness, and shortness of breath.

Muscle Tension

Anxiety often leads to increased muscle tension throughout the body. This reflexive response helps prepare the body for potential physical exertion or defensive maneuvers but can contribute to discomfort, fatigue, and pain if sustained.

Sweating

Anxiety can induce sweating as the body attempts to regulate its temperature in anticipation of exertion. Sweating can occur even in the absence of physical activity due to the activation of the stress response.

Digestive Disturbances

Anxiety can affect the digestive system, leading to symptoms such as stomachaches, nausea, diarrhea, or constipation. This is due to changes in blood flow and the release of stress hormones that can disrupt normal digestive processes.

Immune System Suppression

Prolonged or chronic anxiety may suppress the immune system, making individuals more susceptible to infections and illnesses. This occurs as a result of the prolonged release of stress hormones, which can have immunosuppressive effects.

Overall, the physiological impact of anxiety reflects the body's adaptive response to perceived threats. While these responses are intended to enhance survival in the face of danger, chronic or excessive anxiety can have detrimental effects on physical health and well-being. Understanding the physiological manifestations of anxiety can help individuals recognize and manage their symptoms effectively.

Anxiety Disorders

Anxiety disorders encompass a diverse spectrum of mental health conditions, each characterized by excessive or disproportionate levels of anxiety that interfere with daily life. Let's delve into the key features of some common anxiety disorders:

Generalized Anxiety Disorder (GAD)

GAD involves persistent and excessive worry about a wide range of everyday events and activities. Individuals with GAD often find it challenging to control their worries, which can lead to physical symptoms such as muscle tension, fatigue, irritability, and difficulty concentrating.

Panic Disorder

Panic disorder is marked by recurrent panic attacks—sudden episodes of intense fear or discomfort that reach a peak within minutes. Panic attacks may be accompanied by physical symptoms such as rapid heartbeat, sweating, trembling, shortness of breath, chest pain, or feelings of impending doom. Fear of experiencing another panic attack can lead to avoidance behaviors and may significantly impact daily functioning.

Social Anxiety Disorder (SAD)

SAD, also known as social phobia, involves an intense fear of social situations or performance situations where individuals fear being scrutinized, judged, or embarrassed by others. People with SAD may experience anxiety in a variety of social settings, including public speaking, meeting new people, or attending social gatherings. Avoidance of social situations and fear of negative evaluation are hallmark features of SAD.

Specific Phobias

Specific phobias are irrational and intense fears of specific objects, animals, situations, or activities. Common examples include fear of heights (acrophobia), fear of spiders (arachnophobia), fear of flying (aviophobia), and fear of enclosed spaces (claustrophobia). People with specific phobias may go to great lengths to avoid the feared object or situation, leading to significant impairment in daily functioning.

Obsessive-Compulsive Disorder (OCD)

OCD is characterized by intrusive, unwanted thoughts or obsessions that lead to repetitive behaviors or mental rituals known as compulsions. Obsessions typically evoke feelings of anxiety, disgust, or unease, while compulsions are performed in an attempt to alleviate distress or prevent perceived harm. Common obsessions include fears of contamination, harm, or symmetry, while compulsions may involve rituals such as handwashing, checking, or counting.

Post-Traumatic Stress Disorder (PTSD)

PTSD can develop after exposure to a traumatic event, such as combat, natural disasters, physical or sexual assault, or witnessing a traumatic event. Symptoms may include intrusive memories, flashbacks, nightmares, hypervigilance, avoidance of reminders of the trauma, and changes in mood or cognition. PTSD can significantly impair daily functioning and quality of life.

Agoraphobia

Agoraphobia involves a fear of situations or places where escape may be difficult or embarrassing, such as crowded spaces, public transportation, or open spaces. Individuals with agoraphobia may avoid leaving their homes or may require a companion when venturing outside. Fear of experiencing panic attacks or being unable to escape from perceived threats is a common feature of agoraphobia.

Understanding the nuances of each anxiety disorder is crucial for accurate diagnosis and effective treatment. If you or someone you know is experiencing symptoms of an anxiety disorder, it's essential to seek support from a mental health professional for proper evaluation and guidance.

Anxiety in the Modern World

Anxiety in today's world is something many of us grapple with, and the numbers show just how prevalent it has become. According to various studies and reports, anxiety disorders affect a significant portion of the population, with estimates hovering around 3.8%. But behind these statistics are real people, each navigating their own unique struggles with anxiety in a rapidly changing world.

Modern life presents a host of stressors that can contribute to feelings of anxiety. The fast-paced nature of our society, coupled with increasing demands at work, school, and home, can leave many feeling overwhelmed and on edge. The constant pressure to perform, meet deadlines, and juggle multiple responsibilities can take a toll on our mental health and well-being.

Technology and social media, while offering unprecedented connectivity and convenience, also play a role in exacerbating anxiety. The constant barrage of information, notifications, and comparisons on social media platforms can fuel feelings of inadequacy, FOMO (fear of missing out), and self-doubt. The pressure to curate the perfect image and keep up with the seemingly flawless lives of others can leave us feeling anxious and disconnected from reality.

Moreover, the 24/7 nature of technology means that many of us are never truly able to disconnect and unwind. The blurring of boundaries between work and personal life, along with the expectation of constant availability, can lead to chronic stress and anxiety.

In this modern landscape, it's more important than ever to prioritize our mental health and well-being. Finding balance in our lives, setting boundaries with technology, and cultivating meaningful connections with others are essential steps in managing anxiety in the digital age. By recognizing the impact of our modern lifestyle on anxiety and taking proactive steps to address it, we can work towards creating a healthier and more balanced relationship with ourselves and the world around us.

The Body's Alarm System

The body's alarm system- a mechanism deeply ingrained in our biology- plays a crucial role in our response to perceived threats.

How Does the "Fight or Flight" Response Work?

The fight or flight response is a primal, innate reaction designed to prepare our bodies to deal with perceived threats or dangers. When we encounter a threat—whether it's a physical threat, such as facing a predator, or a psychological threat, like a looming deadline—our bodies undergo a series of rapid physiological changes to help us either confront the threat or escape from it. Here's how it works:

Perception of Threat

The process begins with the perception of a threat by the brain. This can happen through various sensory inputs, such as seeing a potential danger, hearing a loud noise, or experiencing a stressful situation.

Activation of the Hypothalamus

Once the brain detects a threat, it sends signals to the hypothalamus, a region of the brain responsible for regulating various bodily functions, including the stress response.

Release of Stress Hormones

In response to the signals from the brain, the hypothalamus activates the sympathetic nervous system, which triggers the release of stress hormones, primarily adrenaline and cortisol, from the adrenal glands located above the kidneys.

Physiological Changes

Adrenaline rapidly increases heart rate, blood pressure, and respiration rate, preparing the body for action. Blood is redirected away from non-essential organs, such as the digestive system, and toward vital organs, muscles, and the brain to fuel the body's response. Cortisol increases glucose levels in the bloodstream to provide a quick energy source for muscles.

Heightened Sensory Perception

The fight or flight response also enhances sensory perception, making us more alert and aware of our surroundings. Our senses become sharper, allowing us to detect potential threats more quickly.

Activation of Muscles

Muscles tense up and become primed for action, ready to either fight off the threat or flee from it. This increased muscle tension can enhance strength and speed, enabling us to respond effectively to the perceived danger.

Suppression of Non-Essential Functions

Non-essential bodily functions, such as digestion, reproduction, and immune function, are temporarily suppressed during the fight or flight response. This allows the body to conserve energy and focus its resources on dealing with the immediate threat.

Overall, the fight or flight response is a finely tuned survival mechanism that enables us to react swiftly and effectively in the face of danger. While it's essential for our survival, chronic activation of the fight or flight response due to ongoing stressors can have detrimental effects on our physical and mental health. Learning to manage stress and cultivate relaxation techniques can help mitigate the long-term impact of chronic stress on our well-being.

Role of the Amygdala

The amygdala plays a central role in the body's alarm system by processing emotional stimuli and coordinating the physiological response to perceived threats. Situated deep within the brain's temporal lobe, the amygdala consists of two almond-shaped clusters of neurons and is interconnected with various brain regions involved in emotion regulation, memory, and decision-making.

When we encounter a potential threat, sensory information from our environment is relayed to the amygdala for processing. This can include visual, auditory, olfactory, and tactile cues that signal danger. The amygdala then evaluates these sensory inputs, determining whether they represent a threat and warrant a response.

If the amygdala perceives a threat, it triggers a rapid cascade of physiological changes through its connections with other brain regions and the autonomic nervous system. It sends signals to activate the sympathetic nervous system, leading to the release of stress hormones such as adrenaline and cortisol. These hormones prepare the body for action by increasing heart rate, respiration rate, and blood pressure, while redirecting blood flow to muscles and the brain.

Additionally, the amygdala plays a crucial role in forming and storing emotional memories associated with threatening or aversive experiences. It helps to encode and consolidate memories of past threats, allowing us to recognize and respond to similar situations more effectively in the future. This process of associative learning contributes to the amygdala's role in fear conditioning and shaping behavioral responses to potential dangers.

Furthermore, the amygdala interacts closely with higher brain regions involved in cognitive appraisal and decision-making, such as the prefrontal cortex. It helps to integrate emotional information with cognitive evaluations of risk and reward, influencing our perceptions, judgments, and behavioral responses to threatening stimuli.

Overall, the amygdala serves as a key hub in the body's alarm system, orchestrating the physiological and behavioral responses to perceived threats. Its intricate connections with other brain regions allow it to rapidly assess and respond to emotional stimuli, helping us navigate potentially dangerous situations and ensure our survival.

What are the Long-term Effects of an Overactive Internal Alarm System?

An overactive alarm system, characterized by chronic activation of the body's stress response, can have significant long-term effects on both physical and mental health. Here are some potential consequences:

Chronic Stress

Prolonged activation of the stress response can lead to chronic stress, which has been linked to a range of health problems, including cardiovascular disease, hypertension, and diabetes. Chronic stress can also weaken the immune system, making individuals more susceptible to infections and illnesses.

Cardiovascular Issues

Persistent elevation of stress hormones such as adrenaline and cortisol can contribute to cardiovascular issues such as high blood pressure, heart disease, and atherosclerosis (hardening of the arteries). Chronic stress has been associated with an increased risk of heart attacks and strokes.

Digestive Problems

Chronic stress can disrupt digestive processes, leading to gastrointestinal issues such as irritable bowel syndrome (IBS), indigestion, and acid reflux. Stress-related changes in gut function can exacerbate existing digestive conditions and contribute to symptoms such as abdominal pain, bloating, and diarrhea.

Immune System Dysfunction

Prolonged stress can suppress the immune system, making individuals more susceptible to infections and impairing the body's ability to fight off illnesses. Chronic stress has been linked to increased susceptibility to viral infections, autoimmune disorders, and delayed wound healing.

Mental Health Disorders

Chronic stress and an overactive alarm system are closely linked to the development of mental health disorders such as anxiety, depression, and post-traumatic stress disorder (PTSD). Persistent feelings of worry, apprehension, and hypervigilance can lead to emotional exhaustion, burnout, and impaired cognitive function over time.

Sleep Disturbances

Chronic stress can disrupt sleep patterns and contribute to sleep disturbances such as insomnia, restless sleep, and frequent awakenings during the night. Sleep disturbances, in turn, can exacerbate stress levels and impair overall health and well-being.

Cognitive Impairment

Chronic stress can impair cognitive function and memory due to its effects on the brain's hippocampus and prefrontal cortex. Persistent stress can lead to difficulties with concentration, attention, and decision-making, as well as memory problems and cognitive decline over time.

Overall, an overactive alarm system and chronic stress can have profound and far-reaching effects on physical and mental health. Managing stress levels, practicing relaxation techniques, and seeking support from healthcare professionals can help mitigate the long-term impact of chronic stress on overall well-being.

In this chapter, we began our journey into the intricate world of anxiety, exploring its definitions, physiological impacts, and prevalence in the modern world. We gained insights into the body's alarm system, understanding how the fight or flight response works and the pivotal role of the amygdala in orchestrating our physiological and emotional responses to perceived threats.

Furthermore, we examined the various anxiety disorders, recognizing their diverse manifestations and the profound impact they can have on individuals' lives. From generalized anxiety disorder to panic disorder, social anxiety disorder, and beyond, each disorder presents unique challenges and complexities that warrant understanding and empathy.

As we navigated through statistics on anxiety prevalence and explored the role of modern lifestyle factors such as technology and social media, we gained a deeper appreciation for the complexities of anxiety in today's world. The fast-paced nature of modern life, coupled with increasing stressors and societal pressures, underscores the importance of prioritizing mental health and well-being.

In closing, while anxiety may seem daunting and overwhelming at times, it's essential to remember that there is hope and support available. By understanding the nature of anxiety, recognizing its triggers, and developing coping strategies, we can begin to navigate its complexities with resilience and compassion. As we continue our journey, let us embrace the power of safe spaces and the transformative potential they hold in fostering healing, connection, and growth.

Recognizing Your Anxiety Triggers

"To conquer fear is the beginning of wisdom."

- Bertrand Russell

Welcome to Chapter 2 of our exploration into the realm of safe spaces and anxiety management. In this chapter, we will delve into the crucial process of mapping your anxiety triggers. Understanding what triggers your anxiety is a foundational step in developing effective coping strategies and cultivating resilience. We'll explore various techniques and insights to help you identify, understand, and manage your anxiety triggers with greater clarity and confidence.

Common Anxiety Triggers

Common, universal anxiety triggers encompass a range of situations, events, or thoughts that provoke feelings of unease, worry, or fear across individuals. While the specific triggers may vary from person to person, certain themes emerge as widely experienced sources of anxiety. Here are some common, universal anxiety triggers:

Uncertainty

The unpredictability of future outcomes and the inability to control or predict events can trigger feelings of anxiety and apprehension. Uncertainty about the future, such as job stability, health concerns, or relationships, can lead to heightened stress levels and rumination.

Change

Transitions, transitions, and upheavals in life can disrupt familiar routines and challenge one's sense of stability and security. Major life changes such as moving to a new city, starting a new job, or experiencing a significant loss can evoke feelings of anxiety as individuals navigate the unknown.

Social Situations

Interactions with others, particularly in unfamiliar or high-pressure social situations, can trigger anxiety for many people. Social anxiety disorder, characterized by fear of judgment or embarrassment in social settings, may be triggered by situations such as public speaking, meeting new people, or attending social gatherings.

Performance Pressure

The pressure to perform well in academic, professional, or personal endeavors can trigger anxiety in individuals striving for perfection or fearing failure. Performance anxiety may arise in situations such as exams, job interviews, presentations, or athletic competitions.

Health Concerns

Worries about one's health or the health of loved ones can be a significant source of anxiety, particularly in times of illness or uncertainty. Concerns about physical symptoms, medical tests, or chronic health conditions can contribute to heightened stress levels and hypervigilance.

Financial Stress

Economic instability, debt, and financial insecurity can trigger anxiety about one's financial future and ability to meet basic needs. Concerns about job loss, retirement savings, or unexpected expenses can lead to persistent worry and stress.

Existential Concerns

Questions about the meaning of life, mortality, and existential themes can provoke existential anxiety—a profound sense of dread or unease about the nature of existence and the human condition. Contemplating themes such as death, purpose, and identity may trigger existential angst in individuals grappling with existential questions.

Conflict or Confrontation

Confrontation or conflict with others, whether in personal relationships, the workplace, or social settings, can trigger feelings of anxiety and stress. Fear of conflict, rejection, or confrontation may lead individuals to avoid or withdraw from challenging situations.

Environmental Stressors

Environmental factors such as noise, overcrowding, or chaotic surroundings can contribute to feelings of anxiety and overwhelm. Sensory overload or exposure to unpleasant environmental stimuli may trigger stress responses in sensitive individuals.

Media Exposure

Exposure to distressing or alarming news, images, or media content can trigger feelings of anxiety and distress. Constant exposure to negative or sensationalized media coverage of crises, disasters, or conflicts can contribute to heightened anxiety levels and a sense of helplessness.

These common, universal anxiety triggers highlight the diverse range of stressors that individuals may encounter in daily life. Recognizing and acknowledging these triggers is an essential step in managing anxiety effectively and cultivating resilience in the face of life's challenges.

Anxiety Triggers Vary from One Person to Another

While it is true that there are some universal anxiety triggers that we all face, it's important to understand that triggers vary from one person to another.

Triggers can vary significantly from one person to another due to individual differences in experiences, beliefs, personality traits, and sensitivities. While certain triggers may be universally recognized as anxiety-inducing, such as uncertainty or social situations, the specific circumstances or stimuli that provoke anxiety can vary widely based on individual factors. Here's how triggers can vary from person to person:

Personal Experiences

Past experiences play a significant role in shaping their anxiety triggers. Events or situations that have been associated with stress, trauma, or negative emotions in the past may become triggers for anxiety. For example, someone who has experienced a traumatic car accident may develop a fear of driving or being in vehicles, while others may not share the same fear due to different life experiences.

Beliefs and Values

Personal beliefs, values, and perceptions influence how individuals interpret and respond to potential threats or stressors. For example, someone who holds perfectionistic beliefs may be triggered by situations that challenge their sense of control or perfection, such as making mistakes or receiving criticism. Conversely, individuals with a more flexible or resilient mindset may be less affected by similar situations.

Personality Traits

Individual differences in personality traits can influence susceptibility to certain anxiety triggers. For example, individuals who are highly sensitive or neurotic may be more prone to experiencing anxiety in response to stressors, whereas those who are more extroverted or emotionally stable may exhibit greater resilience in the face of adversity.

Cultural Influences

Cultural norms, values, and social expectations can shape individuals' perceptions of stress and anxiety triggers. What may be considered a source of anxiety in one culture may not hold the same significance in another. Cultural differences in coping styles, social support systems, and attitudes toward mental health may also impact how individuals respond to anxiety triggers.

Developmental Stage

Age and developmental stage can influence the types of triggers that individuals are susceptible to. Children and adolescents may be more sensitive to triggers related to academic performance, social acceptance, or family dynamics, whereas adults may experience anxiety triggers related to work, relationships, or existential concerns.

Health and Well-being

Physical health, mental health, and overall well-being can influence vulnerability to anxiety triggers. Individuals experiencing chronic health conditions, chronic pain, or mental health disorders may be more susceptible to anxiety triggers related to health concerns or symptoms. Similarly, stressors such as sleep deprivation, poor nutrition, or lack of exercise can exacerbate anxiety symptoms and increase susceptibility to triggers.

Overall, the variability in anxiety triggers underscores the importance of personalized approaches to anxiety management and treatment. By understanding the unique factors that contribute to individual anxiety triggers, individuals can develop tailored coping strategies and interventions to effectively manage their anxiety and improve overall well-being.

Mapping Your Anxiety Triggers

Understanding and identifying your anxiety triggers is a crucial step in managing anxiety effectively. By recognizing the specific situations, thoughts, or experiences that provoke feelings of anxiety, you can develop targeted strategies to cope with and reduce their impact on your well-being. In this section, we'll explore practical techniques for mapping your anxiety triggers and gaining insight into their underlying causes.

Identifying Your Anxiety Triggers

Identifying your anxiety triggers involves self-awareness and observation of your thoughts, emotions, and reactions in various situations. Pay attention to moments when you feel anxious and ask yourself what preceded those feelings. Reflect on specific situations, events, or thoughts that may have triggered your anxiety. Keep in mind that triggers can be external (e.g., certain situations or environments) or internal (e.g., negative thoughts or memories).

Identifying your personal anxiety triggers involves a process of self-awareness, observation, and reflection. Here are some steps to help you identify your anxiety triggers:

Pay Attention to Your Emotions

Start by paying close attention to your emotions and physical sensations throughout the day. Notice when you start to feel anxious and try to identify the thoughts, situations, or events that preceded those feelings.

Keep a Journal

Keeping an anxiety journal can be a helpful tool for tracking your triggers. Take some time each day to jot down any instances of anxiety you experience, including the trigger, your thoughts and emotions, and any physical sensations you notice. Look for patterns or common themes that emerge over time.

Notice Changes in Your Body

Anxiety often manifests physically as well as emotionally. Pay attention to any physical sensations you experience when you feel anxious, such as a racing heart, shallow breathing, muscle tension, or stomach discomfort. These physical cues can provide valuable clues about your triggers.

Reflect on Past Experiences

Reflect on past experiences of anxiety and try to identify any common triggers that may have contributed to those episodes. Think about specific situations, events, or thoughts that have triggered anxiety in the past and consider whether similar triggers are present in your current life.

Consider Different Categories of Triggers

Anxiety triggers can be categorized in various ways, including situational triggers (e.g., public speaking, social events), cognitive triggers (e.g., negative thoughts, worries), interpersonal triggers (e.g., conflicts with others, relationship stress), and physiological triggers (e.g., caffeine, lack of sleep). Consider each of these categories as you identify your triggers.

Seek Input from Others

Sometimes, it can be helpful to get input from trusted friends, family members, or mental health professionals. They may be able to offer insights or observations that you hadn't considered on your own.

Be Patient and Persistent

Identifying your anxiety triggers is a process that takes time and patience. Be gentle with yourself and acknowledge that it may take some trial and error to identify all of your triggers. Stay persistent and committed to self-awareness and reflection.

By taking these steps to identify your personal anxiety triggers, you can gain valuable insights into the underlying causes of your anxiety and develop targeted strategies for managing it effectively. Remember that everyone's triggers are unique, so what works for one person may not work for another. Trust your own intuition and experiences as you navigate this process.

Tips for Keeping an Anxiety Journal

Keeping an anxiety journal can be a valuable tool for tracking your anxiety triggers, thoughts, and emotions, as well as monitoring your progress in managing anxiety. Here are some tips for keeping an anxiety journal effectively:

Choose a Format

Decide on a format that works best for you. You can use a traditional notebook, a digital journaling app, or even a simple document on your computer or smartphone. Choose a format that feels comfortable and accessible to you.

Set Aside Time

Set aside dedicated time each day to write in your anxiety journal. This could be in the morning to reflect on your goals for the day, in the evening to review your day and unwind, or any other time that works best for you.

Be Consistent

Consistency is key when keeping an anxiety journal. Aim to write in your journal regularly, ideally every day or at least several times a week. Consistent journaling will help you track patterns and trends in your anxiety over time.

Be Honest and Open

Be honest and open in your journal entries. Don't censor yourself or worry about grammar or spelling—just let your thoughts flow freely onto the page. Your journal is a safe space for you to express yourself without judgment.

Include Details

Include as much detail as possible in your journal entries. Describe the situation or trigger that caused your anxiety, the thoughts and emotions you experienced, any physical sensations you noticed, and how you responded to the anxiety. The more detailed your entries, the more insight you'll gain into your anxiety triggers and patterns.

Use Prompts

If you're not sure what to write about, consider using prompts to get started. You can find journaling prompts online or create your own based on your specific goals and interests. Prompts can help stimulate your thinking and provide direction for your journal entries.

Review and Reflect

Periodically review your journal entries and reflect on your experiences. Look for patterns or common themes in your anxiety triggers and responses. Consider what strategies have been helpful in managing your anxiety and what areas you may need to focus on more.

Celebrate Progress

Celebrate your progress and achievements as you work on managing your anxiety. Use your journal to track your successes, no matter how small, and acknowledge the steps you've taken towards greater well-being.

Be Patient

Remember that managing anxiety is a journey, and progress may take time. Be patient with yourself and trust the process. Your anxiety journal is a valuable tool for self-discovery and growth, so keep writing and exploring your experiences.

By following these tips, you can make the most of your anxiety journal and gain valuable insights into your anxiety triggers and how to manage them effectively.

Strategies for Managing Anxiety Triggers

When it comes to dealing with anxiety triggers, it's essential to have a toolkit of strategies to help navigate challenging situations. Here are some practical techniques that can help you manage exposure to triggers:

Gradual Exposure

Think of gradual exposure like dipping your toes into the water before diving in. Start by exposing yourself to anxiety-provoking situations in small, manageable doses. For example, if social situations trigger your anxiety, you might start by attending a small gathering with close friends before gradually working your way up to larger events. By taking things slowly and building up your tolerance over time, you can increase your confidence and reduce the intensity of your anxiety reactions.

Relaxation Techniques

When anxiety strikes, relaxation techniques can be your saving grace. Take a few deep breaths, focusing on the sensation of the air entering and leaving your lungs. Try progressive muscle relaxation, where you systematically tense and then relax different muscle groups in your body, releasing tension and promoting relaxation. Or, immerse yourself in mindfulness meditation, where you bring your attention to the present moment, letting go of worries about the past or future. These techniques can help calm your mind and body, allowing you to approach anxiety triggers with greater ease and composure.

Grounding Techniques

Grounding techniques can help anchor you in the present moment, providing a sense of stability and control when anxiety threatens to overwhelm you. Tune into your senses by focusing on what you can see, hear, touch, taste, and smell in your environment. Notice the texture of the ground beneath your feet, the sound of birds chirping outside, or the warmth of the sun on your skin. Engage in activities that distract your mind from anxious thoughts, such as listening to music, going for a walk in nature, or doing a puzzle. By redirecting your attention away from your anxiety and towards the here and now, you can regain a sense of balance and perspective.

Remember, managing exposure to anxiety triggers is not about avoiding them altogether, but rather about developing healthy coping mechanisms to navigate them with confidence and resilience. Experiment with these techniques to see which ones work best for you, and don't be afraid to reach out for support if you need it. You're not alone in this journey, and with time and practice, you can learn to face your anxiety triggers with courage and grace.

How to Develop Coping Mechanisms to Manage Anxiety Triggers

Developing coping mechanisms to deal with anxiety triggers is a personalized process that involves experimentation, self-awareness, and persistence. Here are some tips to help you develop effective coping mechanisms for managing anxiety triggers:

Identify Your Triggers

Take time to identify and understand your anxiety triggers. Notice patterns in your thoughts, emotions, and behaviors when you experience anxiety. Keep a journal to track your triggers and explore common themes or situations that provoke anxiety.

Educate Yourself

Learn about different coping techniques and strategies for managing anxiety. Research cognitive-behavioral techniques, mindfulness practices, relaxation exercises, and other evidence-based approaches to coping with anxiety. Understanding your options empowers you to choose coping mechanisms that resonate with you.

- Cognitive-Behavioral Techniques: Cognitive-behavioral techniques (CBT) are a cornerstone of therapy for anxiety. CBT focuses on identifying and challenging negative thought patterns and beliefs that contribute to anxiety. By recognizing and reframing distorted thoughts, individuals can change their behavioral responses and reduce anxiety symptoms. Techniques include cognitive restructuring, thought monitoring, and behavioral experiments.

- Mindfulness Practices: Mindfulness involves paying attention to the present moment with openness, curiosity, and acceptance. Mindfulness practices, such as meditation, deep breathing exercises, and body scans, help individuals cultivate awareness of their thoughts, emotions, and bodily sensations without judgment. By practicing mindfulness regularly, individuals can develop greater resilience to stress and anxiety.

- Relaxation Exercises: Relaxation exercises aim to activate the body's relaxation response, counteracting the physiological arousal associated with anxiety. Techniques include deep breathing, progressive muscle relaxation, guided imagery, and autogenic training. These exercises promote physical and mental relaxation, reducing tension and anxiety symptoms.

- Other Evidence-Based Approaches: In addition to CBT, mindfulness, and relaxation techniques, several other evidence-based approaches can help individuals cope with anxiety. These may include exposure therapy, which involves gradually confronting anxiety-provoking situations to desensitize fear responses, and acceptance and commitment therapy (ACT), which focuses on accepting difficult thoughts and feelings while committing to actions aligned with personal values.

Experiment with Different Techniques

Don't be afraid to try out different coping mechanisms to see what works best for you. Experiment with deep breathing exercises, progressive muscle relaxation, visualization techniques, journaling, creative activities, or talking to a supportive friend or therapist. Keep an open mind and be willing to explore new approaches.

Practice Consistently

Consistency is key when it comes to developing coping mechanisms. Set aside time each day to practice your chosen coping techniques, even when you're not feeling anxious. Regular practice helps reinforce your coping skills and makes them more readily available when you need them during moments of heightened anxiety.

Combine Strategies

Combine multiple coping strategies to create a personalized toolkit for managing anxiety triggers. For example, you might use deep breathing exercises to calm your body, cognitive restructuring to challenge negative thoughts, and creative activities to distract your mind from anxious rumination. Experiment with different combinations of techniques to find what works best for you in different situations.

Be Patient and Kind to Yourself

Developing coping mechanisms takes time and patience, so be gentle with yourself as you navigate this process. It's okay to have setbacks or moments of struggle along the way. Celebrate your progress, no matter how small, and acknowledge the effort you're putting into building resilience and managing anxiety.

Seek Support

Don't hesitate to reach out for support from friends, family members, or mental health professionals as you work on developing coping mechanisms for managing anxiety triggers. Talking to others about your experiences can provide validation, encouragement, and practical advice for coping with anxiety.

Stay Open to Learning

Stay open to learning and evolving your coping strategies over time. As you gain more experience with managing anxiety triggers, you may discover new techniques that resonate with you or find that your needs and preferences change. Stay curious and adaptable in your approach to coping with anxiety.

By following these tips and committing to the process of developing coping mechanisms, you can build resilience and empower yourself to effectively manage anxiety triggers in your life. Remember that you have the strength and resources within you to navigate anxiety with courage and grace.

Is Trigger Avoidance a Viable Option for Managing Anxiety?

Avoiding triggers when possible or necessary can be an effective strategy for managing anxiety. Here are some tips for avoiding triggers:

Identify Your Triggers

Take time to identify the specific situations, environments, or stimuli that trigger your anxiety. Keep a journal or make a list of your triggers to help you better understand them.

Create Boundaries

Establish clear boundaries to protect yourself from triggers. This may involve setting limits on certain activities or interactions that consistently provoke anxiety. Learn to say no to situations or commitments that you know will trigger your anxiety.

Plan Ahead

Anticipate situations where you're likely to encounter triggers and plan accordingly. If you know that certain events or environments are anxiety-provoking, consider whether it's possible to avoid them or minimize your exposure.

Modify Your Environment

Make changes to your environment to reduce exposure to triggers. This could involve creating a calming and supportive home environment, avoiding places or situations that exacerbate anxiety, or setting up specific spaces where you feel safe and comfortable.

Practice Self-Care

Prioritize self-care practices that help reduce stress and build resilience. Engage in activities that promote relaxation and well-being, such as exercise, meditation, spending time in nature, or practicing hobbies that bring you joy.

Use Distraction Techniques

When faced with unavoidable triggers, distract yourself with activities or thoughts that shift your focus away from anxiety. Listen to music, watch a movie, read a book, or engage in a creative hobby to distract your mind and reduce anxiety.

Seek Support

Reach out to friends, family members, or mental health professionals for support when dealing with triggers. Having a supportive network of people who understand your triggers and can offer encouragement and guidance can be invaluable in managing anxiety.

Practice Relaxation Techniques

Incorporate relaxation techniques into your daily routine to help manage anxiety when triggers arise. Deep breathing exercises, progressive muscle relaxation, and mindfulness meditation can help calm your mind and body, reducing the impact of triggers on your well-being.

Know Your Limits

Recognize when avoidance becomes a predominant coping strategy and consider whether it's ultimately helpful or harmful in the long run. While it's important to avoid triggers when necessary for your mental health, it's also essential to confront and work through anxiety-provoking situations when possible to build resilience.

Remember that avoiding triggers is just one strategy for managing anxiety and may not always be possible or appropriate. It's essential to develop a comprehensive toolkit of coping mechanisms that includes strategies for both avoiding and confronting triggers effectively. Experiment with different approaches to find what works best for you, and don't hesitate to seek professional help if you're struggling to manage anxiety triggers on your own.

As we conclude this chapter, it's important to reflect on what we've learned thus far. We've explored the intricate world of anxiety, from understanding its definitions and physiological impact as well as the prevalence of anxiety in our modern world. We've learned about the body's alarm system and how it can sometimes become overactive, leading to heightened anxiety responses.

We've also discussed the importance of mapping our anxiety triggers, recognizing common triggers, and developing coping mechanisms to manage exposure to triggers effectively. Whether through cognitive-behavioral techniques, mindfulness practices, or relaxation exercises, we've discovered a range of evidence-based approaches for coping with anxiety triggers.

As we move forward, let's remember that managing anxiety is a journey, not a destination. It takes time, patience, and dedication to develop the skills and strategies necessary to navigate life's challenges with resilience and grace. By continuing to explore and practice the coping mechanisms discussed in this chapter, we can empower ourselves to lead more fulfilling and balanced lives, free from the grip of anxiety.

In the chapters ahead, we'll explore the concept of safe spaces and how they can provide comfort, support, and healing in our journey toward emotional well-being. So, take a deep breath, embrace the lessons learned, and know that you're not alone on this path. Together, we'll navigate the complexities of anxiety and discover the power of safe spaces to transform our lives for the better.

Crafting Your Personal Safe Space

"Peace: it does not mean to be in a place where there is no noise, trouble, or hard work. It means to be in the midst of those things and still be calm in your heart."

- Unknown

In this chapter, we'll explore the concept of a safe space and how you can create one that meets your unique needs. From defining what a safe space means to you to exploring the physical and sensory elements that contribute to its comfort, we'll guide you through the process of crafting a sanctuary where you can find solace and rejuvenation.

The Concept of a Safe Space

At the heart of every safe space lies the profound concept of refuge—a sanctuary where one can unfurl their true selves, unencumbered by the weight of judgment or fear. It's a deeply personal haven, tailored to the unique needs and preferences of its inhabitant, where vulnerability is met with compassion, and authenticity is celebrated.

Define What "Safe Space" Means to You

Defining what a safe space means to you personally involves introspection and reflection on your individual needs, preferences, and experiences. Here are some steps to help you define what a safe space means to you:

- Reflect on Your Feelings: Take some time to reflect on your emotions and experiences. Consider situations or environments where you feel most at ease, comfortable, and accepted. Pay attention to how you feel in different settings and with different people.

- Identify Your Triggers: Think about what triggers your anxiety, stress, or discomfort. These triggers can provide valuable insight into the qualities and conditions that contribute to your sense of safety and security.

- Consider Your Needs: Consider what you need in order to feel safe, supported, and respected. This could include physical comfort, emotional validation, privacy, autonomy, or a sense of belonging. Reflect on past experiences where these needs were met or unmet.

- Explore Your Preferences: Explore your preferences for the environment, atmosphere, and dynamics of a safe space. Do you prefer a quiet, secluded space or a bustling, social environment? Are you drawn to natural settings, cozy interiors, or modern design? Think about what elements contribute to your sense of comfort and well-being.

- Evaluate Your Relationships: Consider the role that relationships play in creating a sense of safety and security. Reflect on the people in your life who make you feel valued, understood, and supported. Identify characteristics or behaviors that foster trust, communication, and mutual respect in your relationships.

- Imagine Your Ideal Space: Envision your ideal safe space, taking into account all the elements that contribute to your sense of safety, comfort, and well-being. Visualize the physical environment, the atmosphere, the people involved, and the activities or rituals that take place there.

- Listen to Your Intuition: Trust your instincts and listen to your inner voice. Pay attention to how you feel when you think about different environments or situations. Notice any sensations, emotions, or thoughts that arise, and honor them as valuable indicators of what feels safe and supportive to you.

- Adjust as Needed: Remember that your definition of a safe space may evolve over time as you grow, change, and learn more about yourself. Be open to adjusting your definition and exploring new possibilities as you continue on your journey of self-discovery and personal growth.

By engaging in this process of reflection and self-exploration, you can gain clarity and insight into what a safe space means to you personally. This understanding can guide you in creating environments and relationships that nurture your well-being and support your journey toward greater resilience and fulfillment.

Psychological Benefits of Having a Safe Space

Having a safe space offers a multitude of psychological benefits that contribute to overall well-being and mental health. Some of these benefits include:

Reduced Stress and Anxiety

A safe space provides a refuge from the pressures and stressors of everyday life, allowing individuals to relax, unwind, and recharge. By creating a sense of safety and security, it helps reduce levels of stress and anxiety, promoting a greater sense of calm and peace of mind.

Emotional Regulation

Being in a safe space enables individuals to process and regulate their emotions more effectively. It offers a supportive environment where they can express their feelings without fear of judgment or reprisal, leading to greater emotional awareness and resilience.

Increased Self-Expression

Safe spaces encourage individuals to express themselves authentically and openly without fear of criticism or rejection. This fosters a sense of freedom and empowerment, allowing them to explore their thoughts, feelings, and identity with confidence and authenticity.

Enhanced Self-Esteem

Feeling safe and accepted in a supportive environment can boost self-esteem and self-worth. When individuals are affirmed and validated for who they are, they develop a greater sense of confidence, self-respect, and self-compassion.

Improved Relationships

Safe spaces facilitate positive interactions and communication, fostering deeper connections and mutual understanding among individuals. They provide a platform for healthy relationships to flourish, characterized by trust, empathy, and respect.

Coping and Resilience

Having a safe space equips individuals with coping mechanisms and resources to navigate life's challenges more effectively. It serves as a buffer against adversity, providing a source of strength and support during difficult times.

Promotion of Mental Health

Safe spaces play a crucial role in promoting mental health and well-being. By offering a sanctuary where individuals can prioritize self-care, seek support, and engage in activities that nourish their mind, body, and spirit, they contribute to overall mental health and resilience.

In essence, safe spaces serve as vital sanctuaries for individuals to find solace, support, and rejuvenation in an often hectic and demanding world. They provide a foundation for emotional growth, healing, and self-discovery, empowering individuals to thrive and flourish in all aspects of their lives.

Examples of Safe Spaces

Safe spaces can vary widely and may include:

- Home: For many people, their home serves as the ultimate safe space—a place where they can relax, unwind, and be themselves without fear of judgment or harm. Within the walls of their home, individuals have control over their environment and can create a space that reflects their values, preferences, and needs.

- Bedroom: Within the home, the bedroom often

becomes a sanctuary—a private retreat where individuals can retreat from the outside world and find solace. Whether it's curling up with a good book, listening to music, or simply enjoying a moment of quiet reflection, the bedroom provides a space for relaxation and rejuvenation.

- Nature: Natural environments such as parks, forests, beaches, and mountains can serve as safe spaces for many people. Immersing oneself in nature can have a calming and grounding effect, allowing individuals to connect with the natural world and find peace amidst the chaos of daily life.

- Therapist's Office: For individuals seeking therapy or counseling, the therapist's office can become a safe space for exploring thoughts, feelings, and experiences in a supportive and nonjudgmental environment. Therapists provide a safe and confidential space where clients can process emotions, gain insight, and work towards personal growth and healing.

- Support Groups: Support groups, whether in-person or online, offer safe spaces for individuals to connect with others who share similar experiences, challenges, or identities. These groups provide a sense of community, understanding, and validation, fostering mutual support and empowerment.

- Art Studios or Creative Spaces: For individuals who find solace in creative expression, art studios, workshops, or creative spaces can serve as safe havens. Engaging in artistic pursuits such as painting, writing, or sculpting allows individuals to express themselves authentically and process their emotions in a creative and therapeutic way.

- Community Centers or Cultural Spaces: Community centers, cultural centers, or other gathering places can provide safe spaces for people to come together, celebrate diversity, and share common interests or identities. These spaces often offer programming, events, or resources that promote inclusivity, belonging, and social connection.

- Virtual Communities: In today's digital age, virtual communities such as online forums, social media groups, or virtual support networks can serve as safe spaces for individuals to connect with others from the comfort of their own homes. These online communities provide a platform for sharing experiences, seeking support, and finding camaraderie with like-minded individuals.

These are just a few examples of safe spaces, and it's important to recognize that what constitutes a safe space can vary greatly from person to person. Ultimately, a safe space is any environment or context where individuals feel accepted, valued, and free to be themselves without fear of judgment or harm.

Choosing & Setting Up Your Safe Space

Creating your personal safe space is a deeply personal and meaningful endeavor. It's about intentionally curating an environment that nurtures your well-being, supports your needs, and reflects your unique preferences and personality. Here's how to choose and set up your personal safe space:

Choosing Your Safe Space Location

When choosing a location for your safe space, consider the following tips to ensure it meets your needs and provides the comfort and support you seek:

- Reflect on Your Preferences: Take some time to reflect on the environments where you feel most at ease and comfortable. Consider whether you prefer quiet, secluded spaces or bustling, social environments. Think about whether you feel more at home indoors or outdoors, and whether you prefer natural or urban settings.

- Consider Privacy: Choose a location that offers a degree of privacy and solitude, where you can retreat from the outside world and find peace and quiet. This could be a spare room in your home, a secluded corner of your garden, or a quiet spot in a nearby park.

- Assess Accessibility: Ensure that your safe space is easily accessible and readily available whenever you need it. Choose a location that is convenient to access, whether it's within your home, workplace, or community. Consider factors such as proximity, transportation, and ease of entry.

- Evaluate Comfort: Pay attention to the physical comfort of the location you choose. Consider factors such as temperature, lighting, seating options, and noise levels. Choose a space that feels comfortable and inviting, where you can relax and unwind without distraction.

- Think About Safety: Prioritize safety when choosing a location for your safe space. Ensure that the environment is free from hazards and potential risks, such as sharp objects, slippery surfaces, or unstable furniture. Choose a location where you feel secure and protected.

- Personalize Your Space: Consider how you can personalize the location to make it feel truly your own. Add personal touches such as photos, artwork, or decorative items that bring you joy and comfort. Make the space reflect your personality and preferences.

- Adaptability: Choose a location that can adapt to your changing needs and circumstances. Consider whether the space can accommodate different activities, moods, or seasons. Choose a location that can evolve along with you as you grow and change.

- Trust Your Instincts: Ultimately, trust your instincts when choosing a location for your safe space. Listen to your intuition and choose a location that feels right for you. Pay attention to how you feel when you're in the space, and trust yourself to make the best decision for your well-being.

By considering these tips and trusting your instincts, you can choose a location for your safe space that provides the comfort, support, and sanctuary you need to thrive. Remember that your safe space is a reflection of you, so make it a place where you feel truly at home.

Elements that Make a Space Comforting

Several factors contribute to making a safe space comforting:

- Physical Comfort: Comfortable seating, soft textures, and ergonomic design contribute to physical comfort in a safe space. Plush cushions, cozy blankets, and supportive furniture help individuals relax and feel at ease.

- Warmth and Coziness: Warm lighting, soft colors, and inviting decor create a cozy atmosphere that promotes relaxation and comfort. Warmth can also be enhanced through tactile elements such as soft fabrics and natural materials like wood and wool.

- Sense of Security: A safe space should provide a sense of security and protection from external stressors. This can be achieved through features such as privacy, controlled access, and a tranquil environment that shields individuals from noise and distractions.

- Emotional Support: Emotional support is a key aspect of a comforting safe space. This can come from trusted individuals who offer understanding, empathy, and validation, as well as from the space itself, which should foster feelings of acceptance, belonging, and non-judgment.

- Personalization: Personal touches and familiar items contribute to a sense of comfort and familiarity in a safe space. Surrounding oneself with items that hold personal significance, such as photos, artwork, or sentimental objects, creates a warm and inviting environment.

- Calming Environment: A safe space should be designed to promote relaxation and reduce stress.

This can be achieved through elements such as soothing colors, natural materials, and calming scents like lavender or chamomile.

- Freedom of Expression: Individuals should feel free to express themselves authentically in a safe space without fear of judgment or criticism. Encouraging self-expression through creative outlets, open communication, and acceptance of diverse perspectives enhances the comfort and inclusivity of the space.

- Positive Associations: Positive associations with the space, such as happy memories or feelings of security, contribute to its comfort. Building positive associations through enjoyable activities, meaningful interactions, and supportive relationships enhances the overall comfort and well-being of individuals in the space.

Overall, a comforting safe space is one that provides physical, emotional, and psychological comfort, fosters a sense of security and belonging, and supports individuals in feeling relaxed, accepted, and at peace. By attending to these elements, individuals can create environments that promote well-being, resilience, and personal growth.

Why is it Important to Personalize Your Safe Space?

Personalizing your safe space is important for several reasons:

- Sense of Ownership: Personalizing your safe space allows you to take ownership of the environment and make it uniquely yours. By adding personal touches and decorative elements that reflect your personality, interests, and preferences, you create a space that feels like an extension of yourself.

- Comfort and Familiarity: Personalization contributes to a sense of comfort and familiarity in your safe space. Surrounding yourself with items that hold personal significance, such as photos, artwork, or sentimental objects, can evoke positive emotions and memories, making the space feel warm and inviting.

- Emotional Connection: Personalizing your safe space fosters an emotional connection to the environment. When you fill your space with items that resonate with you on a deep level, you create a sense of belonging and emotional attachment that enhances your overall well-being.

- Expression of Identity: Your safe space is an opportunity to express your identity and showcase who you are as an individual. Personalizing the space allows you to showcase your unique style, interests, and values, creating a space that reflects your true self and celebrates your individuality.

- Support for Self-Expression: Personalizing your safe space encourages self-expression and creativity. By surrounding yourself with items that inspire you and reflect your passions, you create an environment that supports self-expression and encourages you to explore your interests and talents.

- Stress Reduction: Personalizing your safe space can help reduce stress and promote relaxation. When you fill your space with items that bring you joy and comfort, you create a calming and soothing environment that serves as a refuge from the stresses of daily life.

- Empowerment: Personalizing your safe space empowers you to take control of your environment and create a space that meets your unique needs and preferences. By making intentional choices about how to decorate and arrange your space, you assert agency over your surroundings and cultivate a sense of empowerment.

Overall, personalizing your safe space transforms it from a mere physical environment into a meaningful sanctuary that supports your well-being, fosters self-expression, and reflects your identity and values. By infusing your space with personal touches and meaningful elements, you create a space that feels truly like home—a place where you can be yourself and find solace, comfort, and renewal.

The Sensory Experience

The sensory experience of your safe space plays a crucial role in promoting relaxation, comfort, and emotional well-being. Here's why each aspect is important:

Utilizing Calming Scents

Scents have a powerful impact on our mood, emotions, and overall sense of well-being. Certain aromas, such as lavender, chamomile, or jasmine, have been shown to have calming and stress-relieving effects. By incorporating these calming scents into your safe space, whether through candles, essential oils, or diffusers, you can create an environment that promotes relaxation and soothes the mind.

Selecting Soothing Sounds

Sounds can also have a profound effect on our emotional state and stress levels. Soft, gentle sounds such as nature sounds, instrumental music, or white noise can help mask background noise and promote a sense of tranquility in your safe space. By selecting soothing sounds that resonate with you personally, you can create an auditory environment that fosters relaxation and calm.

Incorporating Comforting Textures

Textures can evoke feelings of comfort, warmth, and security. Soft, tactile materials such as plush blankets, fluffy pillows, or cozy rugs can provide physical comfort and promote a sense of coziness in your safe space. Incorporating comforting textures into your environment can enhance the overall sensory experience and create a space that feels inviting and nurturing.

By paying attention to the sensory experience of your safe space and intentionally selecting elements that promote relaxation and comfort, you can create an environment that supports your emotional well-being and helps you feel calm, grounded, and at ease.

As we conclude this chapter on crafting your personal safe space, it's important to remember the significance of creating an environment that truly nurtures your well-being. By understanding the importance of each element—choosing the right location, incorporating comforting elements, and personalizing the space to reflect your unique preferences—you are taking a meaningful step towards cultivating a sanctuary that supports you in moments of need.

Your safe space isn't just a physical location; it's a reflection of your inner world—a place where you can retreat, recharge, and find solace amidst life's challenges. By engaging your senses with calming scents, soothing sounds, and comforting textures, you're creating an immersive experience that speaks to your soul and promotes relaxation on a profound level.

As you embark on this journey of creating your personal safe space, trust in your instincts and allow yourself to be guided by what brings you joy, comfort, and peace. Whether it's a cozy corner of your home, a tranquil outdoor retreat, or a virtual sanctuary you carry with you wherever you go, know that your safe space is a testament to your resilience, strength, and commitment to self-care.

In the next chapter, we'll explore the transformative power of rituals and routines in nurturing your well-being and enhancing your sense of security and stability. Until then, may your safe space serve as a haven of comfort and renewal, providing you with the refuge and support you need to thrive.

Safe Spaces at Home

"The home should be the treasure chest of living."

- Le Corbusier

Your home is more than just four walls and a roof; it's your personal sanctuary—a place where you can find refuge from the chaos of the outside world, where you find comfort, solace, and belonging. In this chapter, we'll explore how to transform your living space into a sanctuary that nurtures your well-being and promotes relaxation and peace.

Picture this: You step through the front door after a long day, and instantly, a sense of calm washes over you. Your living space welcomes you like an old friend, enveloping you in warmth and tranquility. From the cozy nook where you curl up with a good book to the sun-drenched corner where you practice yoga, every corner of your home is designed with intention and care to support your mental, emotional, and physical well-being.

In this chapter, we will explore the importance of a dedicated relaxation spot, the art of decluttering for mental clarity, and the transformative power of incorporating nature and greenery into your living space. From your bedroom, your ultimate retreat for restful sleep, to communal areas designed for comfort and connection, we'll explore how to create a sanctuary that nourishes your soul and restores your spirit.

Creating a Sanctuary in Your Living Space

In today's fast-paced world, finding moments of peace and tranquility can feel like a luxury. However, within the confines of your own home lies the opportunity to carve out a space dedicated to relaxation and rejuvenation—a sanctuary where you can escape the stresses of daily life and reconnect with yourself.

The Importance of a Dedicated Relaxation Spot

Creating a dedicated relaxation spot within your living space is important for several reasons:

- Promotes Stress Reduction: Having a designated area where you can unwind and relax helps to promote stress reduction. When you enter your relaxation spot, it serves as a signal to your brain that it's time to slow down, pause, and let go of the stresses of the y.

- Encourages Self-Care: Designating a specific space for relaxation encourages you to prioritize self-care. It sends a message to yourself that taking time for relaxation and rejuvenation is essential for your well-being, helping to counteract the tendency to prioritize work or other responsibilities over self-care.

- Fosters Mindfulness: Having a dedicated relaxation spot provides an opportunity to practice mindfulness and presence. Whether you use the space for meditation, reading, or simply quiet reflection, it encourages you to be fully present in the moment, cultivating a sense of calm and awareness.

- Supports Mental Health: Regularly spending time in a relaxation spot can have positive effects on mental health. It provides a refuge from the demands and pressures of daily life, offering a safe space where you can recharge and replenish your mental energy.

- Enhances Overall Well-Being: Creating a dedicated relaxation spot contributes to overall well-being by promoting relaxation, reducing stress, and fostering a sense of balance and harmony in your life. It serves as a sanctuary where you can nurture your body, mind, and spirit, supporting your overall health and happiness.

In essence, a dedicated relaxation spot serves as a physical manifestation of your commitment to self-care and well-being. By intentionally creating a space where you can relax and recharge, you prioritize your mental and emotional health, fostering a greater sense of balance, peace, and resilience in your life.

Decluttering for Mental Clarity

Clutter is often a trigger for anxiety, which means that your safe space should be clutter-free. Benefits of a clutter-free safe space include:

- Promoting Relaxation: Clutter can create visual chaos and make your safe space feel cramped and disorganized. A clutter-free environment, on the other hand, promotes relaxation by creating a sense of openness and tranquility. When your surroundings are free from clutter, you can more easily unwind and destress in your safe space.

- Enhancing Mental Clarity: Clutter can be distracting and overwhelming, making it difficult to focus and think clearly. A clutter-free environment allows for better mental clarity, as fewer distractions are competing for your attention. This clarity of mind can help you better process your thoughts and emotions while in your safe space.

- Reducing Stress and Anxiety: Clutter has been linked to increased levels of stress and anxiety. Living in a cluttered environment can contribute to feelings of overwhelm and make it harder to relax and unwind. By keeping your safe space clutter-free, you create a serene and peaceful environment that promotes calmness and reduces stress.

- Promoting Safety: Cluttered spaces can pose safety hazards, such as tripping over items or difficulty navigating through crowded areas. Keeping your safe space clutter-free reduces the risk of accidents and injuries, allowing you to feel safe and secure in your environment.

- Fostering Positive Energy: A clutter-free environment allows positive energy to flow freely throughout your space. Clutter can block the flow of energy and create stagnant areas that feel heavy and oppressive. By keeping your safe space clutter-free, you create a harmonious and uplifting atmosphere that supports your well-being.

Overall, maintaining a clutter-free safe space is essential for creating a peaceful, relaxing, and harmonious environment where you can feel truly at ease. By decluttering regularly and keeping your space organized, you can enjoy the full benefits of your safe space and nurture your overall sense of well-being.

Making Your Bedroom a Retreat

Creating a bedroom that serves as a safe haven for relaxation and restful sleep involves fostering an environment that promotes tranquility, comfort, and security. Here are some tips to help you achieve this:

- Opt for Comfortable Bedding: Invest in high-quality bedding that feels soft and inviting. Choose sheets, pillows, and blankets made from breathable, natural fabrics like cotton or linen to promote comfort and regulate temperature throughout the night.

- Choose a Comfortable Mattress: Select a mattress that provides adequate support for your body and aligns with your preferred sleep position. Test out different mattress types and firmness levels to find the one that offers optimal comfort and support for a restful night's sleep.

- Create a Relaxing Color Scheme: Choose calming, soothing colors for your bedroom decor, such as soft blues, greens, or neutral tones. These colors can help create a serene atmosphere conducive to relaxation and sleep.

- Minimize Clutter: Keep your bedroom clutter-free to promote a sense of calm and tranquility. Clear surfaces of unnecessary items and invest in storage solutions to keep belongings organized and out of sight.

- Control Light Levels: Create a sleep-friendly environment by controlling light levels in your bedroom. Use blackout curtains or blinds to block out external light sources, and consider using dimmer switches or bedside lamps with adjustable brightness to create a relaxing ambiance.

- Limit Technology: Minimize exposure to screens and electronic devices before bedtime, as the blue light emitted by these devices can disrupt sleep patterns. Create a technology-free zone in your bedroom and establish a relaxing bedtime routine that does not involve screens.

- Incorporate Relaxation Techniques: Establish a calming bedtime routine to signal to your body that it's time to wind down and prepare for sleep. This could include activities such as reading, practicing gentle yoga or meditation, or listening to calming music or nature sounds.

- Maintain a Comfortable Temperature: Keep your bedroom at a comfortable temperature for sleeping, typically between 60 to 67 degrees Fahrenheit (15.5 to 19.5 degrees Celsius). Use fans, air conditioning, or heating as needed to achieve your desired sleep environment.

- Promote Fresh Air and Air Quality: Ensure your bedroom is well-ventilated and maintain good air quality by opening windows regularly, using air purifiers, and keeping indoor plants that can help filter the air.

- Banish Work and Stress: Keep work-related items and reminders of stress out of your bedroom to create a space dedicated solely to rest and relaxation. This helps train your brain to associate the bedroom with sleep rather than stress or productivity.

By incorporating these tips into your bedroom design and nightly routine, you can create a safe haven that promotes relaxation and restful sleep, allowing you to enjoy the benefits of a peaceful night's rest and wake up feeling refreshed and rejuvenated each morning.

Tips for Establishing a Calming Pre-Sleep Routine

Establishing a calming pre-sleep routine can help signal to your body that it's time to wind down and prepare for restful sleep. Here are some steps you can take to create a soothing bedtime ritual:

- Set a Consistent Bedtime: Aim to go to bed and wake up at the same time every day, even on weekends. Consistency helps regulate your body's internal clock and can improve the quality of your sleep over time.

- Limit Screen Time: Minimize exposure to screens and electronic devices at least an hour before bed time. The blue light emitted by screens can interfere with your body's natural sleep-wake cycle, making it harder to fall asleep. Instead, opt for screen-free activities such as reading, journaling, or practicing relaxation techniques.

- Practice Relaxation Techniques: Incorporate relaxation techniques into your pre-sleep routine to help calm your mind and body. This could include deep breathing exercises, progressive muscle relaxation, or guided meditation. Experiment with different techniques to find what works best for you.

- Take a Warm Bath or Shower: A warm bath or shower can help relax your muscles and promote feelings of relaxation and drowsiness. Adding calming essential oils such as lavender or chamomile to your bath can enhance the soothing effects.

- Engage in Gentle Stretching: Gentle stretching exercises can help release tension from your muscles and prepare your body for sleep. Focus on stretches that target areas of tension, such as the neck, shoulders, and lower back.

- Create a Relaxing Environment: Make your bedroom a peaceful and comfortable environment conducive to sleep. Dim the lights, adjust the temperature to a comfortable level, and remove any distractions that may disrupt your sleep, such as noise or clutter.

- Avoid Stimulants: Avoid consuming stimulants such as caffeine and nicotine in the hours leading up to bedtime, as they can interfere with your ability to fall asleep. Instead, opt for caffeine-free herbal teas or warm milk, which can promote relaxation and drowsiness.

- Practice Gratitude: Take a few moments before bed to reflect on the positives of your day and express gratitude for the things you are thankful for. Cultivating a sense of gratitude can help shift your focus away from worries or stressors and promote feelings of contentment and peace.

- Establish a Bedtime Ritual: Develop a consistent bedtime ritual that you perform each night before sleep. This could include activities such as brushing your teeth, washing your face, and reading a book or listening to calming music. Over time, your body will come to associate these rituals with sleep, making it easier to drift off at bedtime.

By incorporating these calming pre-sleep activities into your nightly routine, you can help prepare your mind and body for restful sleep and improve the quality of your sleep overall. Experiment with different techniques to find what works best for you and be patient as you establish a routine that supports your sleep health.

How to Create a Calm Atmosphere in Shared Spaces

When it comes to creating a calm atmosphere in shared spaces, fostering harmony and respecting each other's needs and preferences is essential. Here are some tips to help you establish a peaceful environment that promotes relaxation and well-being for all house members:

- Organizing for Harmony: Collaborate with your housemates to organize shared spaces in a way that accommodates everyone's needs and promotes harmony. Keep communication lines open and be willing to compromise on matters such as furniture arrangement, storage solutions, and room aesthetics. By working together, you can create a space that feels comfortable and inviting for everyone.

- Establish Tech-Free Zones: Designate certain areas of your home as tech-free zones where electronic devices are not allowed. This could include the dining area, living room, or designated relaxation spaces. Encourage house members to unplug and disconnect from screens during designated times, allowing for more meaningful interactions and promoting relaxation without the distractions of technology.

- Create Cozy Gathering Spaces: Design shared spaces with comfort and relaxation in mind. Incorporate cozy seating areas, soft lighting, and comfortable furnishings to create inviting spaces where house members can gather, unwind, and connect with each other. Consider adding elements such as throw pillows, blankets, and area rugs to enhance the coziness of these spaces.

- Respect Each Other's Privacy: Respect each other's need for privacy and personal space within shared areas. Establish boundaries and guidelines for respecting personal belongings and private spaces, and encourage open communication to address any concerns or conflicts that may arise. By creating a culture of mutual respect and consideration, you can foster a sense of safety and security within your shared living environment.

- Encourage Open Communication: Encourage open and honest communication among house members to address any issues or conflicts that may arise. Establish regular check-ins or house meetings where everyone has the opportunity to voice their concerns, share feedback, and work together to find solutions. By fostering a culture of open communication and collaboration, you can create a supportive and harmonious living environment where everyone feels valued and respected.

By implementing these strategies, you can create a calm and harmonious atmosphere in shared spaces that promotes relaxation, well-being, and positive relationships among house members. Remember to prioritize open communication, mutual respect, and consideration for each other's needs and preferences to create a living environment where everyone feels comfortable and at ease.

As we wrap up this chapter, it's clear that creating a peaceful and welcoming atmosphere in shared spaces is vital. By organizing thoughtfully, setting up tech-free areas, and keeping communication open, you've made strides in fostering an environment where relaxation, connection, and overall well-being can thrive among all house members.

In the next chapter, we'll delve into the importance of self-care practices in nurturing your physical, emotional, and mental health. Join us as we explore how prioritizing self-care can lead to a life filled with balance, vitality, and fulfillment.

Establishing Boundaries for a Safe Work Environment

"Balance is not something you find, it's something you create."

- Jana Kingsford

In the fast-paced and demanding world of work, establishing boundaries is crucial for maintaining a healthy and productive environment, as well as mitigating anxiety. In this chapter, we'll explore how to set boundaries with colleagues, personalize your workspace, and achieve a healthy work-life balance.

The Importance of Personalizing Your Workspace

Personalizing your workspace is important for several reasons, as it can significantly impact your overall well-being, productivity, and job satisfaction.

Firstly, personalizing your workspace creates a sense of ownership and belonging. When you add elements of your personality, such as photos, artwork, or decorative items, to your desk or office, it transforms the space into a reflection of who you are. This can help you feel more connected to your work environment and increase your sense of pride and investment in your job.

Moreover, a personalized workspace can enhance your comfort and morale. Surrounding yourself with familiar and comforting items from home can create a sense of warmth and familiarity, making the work environment feel more inviting and enjoyable. This can help reduce feelings of stress and anxiety, making it easier to focus and stay motivated throughout the day.

Additionally, personalizing your workspace can boost creativity and inspiration. By surrounding yourself with items that inspire you or evoke positive emotions, you can create an environment that encourages creativity and innovation. This can lead to greater job satisfaction and fulfillment, as well as increased productivity and effectiveness in your work.

Furthermore, a personalized workspace can improve organization and efficiency. When you have a designated place for everything and your desk is organized according to your preferences, it becomes easier to find what you need and stay on top of tasks. This can streamline your workflow and minimize distractions, allowing you to work more efficiently and effectively.

Overall, personalizing your workspace is essential for creating a supportive and conducive environment that enhances your well-being, productivity, and job satisfaction. By adding personal touches, organizing your space to suit your needs, and surrounding yourself with items that inspire and motivate you, you can create a workspace that feels like your own and enables you to thrive professionally.

Tips for Personalizing Your Workspace

Personalizing your workspace is a great way to make your work environment feel more comfortable, inviting, and conducive to productivity. Here are some tips on how to personalize your workspace:

- Add Personal Touches: Incorporate items that reflect your personality, interests, and values into your workspace. This could include photographs of loved ones, artwork, motivational quotes, or mementos from meaningful experiences. Surrounding yourself with familiar and meaningful items can create a sense of warmth and familiarity in your workspace.

- Choose Decorative Elements: Select decorative elements such as plants, desk accessories, or decorative lighting to add visual interest and personality to your workspace. Choose items that resonate with you and make you feel happy and inspired when you look at them.

- Organize Thoughtfully: Keep your workspace organized and clutter-free to create a more efficient and functional environment. Invest in storage solutions such as desk organizers, file holders, and shelving units to keep your belongings neatly arranged and easily accessible. A tidy workspace can help reduce stress and increase productivity.

- Personalize Your Technology: Customize your computer desktop background, screensaver, and phone wallpaper with images or quotes that inspire you. You can also personalize your digital workspace with productivity tools and apps that suit your preferences and workflow.

- Create a Comfortable Work Environment: Pay attention to ergonomics and comfort when setting up your workspace. Invest in a comfortable chair, supportive keyboard and mouse, and ergonomic desk setup to reduce strain and discomfort during long periods of work.

- Incorporate Color: Choose colors for your workspace that evoke positive emotions and energy. Consider incorporating calming hues such as blues and greens for a sense of tranquility, or vibrant colors such as yellows and oranges for a boost of energy and creativity.

- Make it Functional: Personalize your workspace to suit your specific needs and preferences. Arrange your desk layout in a way that optimizes workflow and efficiency. Keep frequently used items within easy reach, and designate specific areas for different tasks to minimize distractions and maximize focus.

- Create Zones: Establish different zones within your workspace for specific activities, such as a designated area for focused work, a relaxation corner for breaks, and a space for collaboration or brainstorming. This can help create a sense of balance and versatility in your workspace.

By incorporating these tips, you can personalize your workspace to create a comfortable, inspiring, and functional environment that supports your productivity and well-being. Experiment with different elements and arrangements to find what works best for you, and enjoy the benefits of a personalized workspace tailored to your needs and preferences.

The Importance of a Quiet Zone

Establishing a "quiet zone" in your workspace is important for several reasons:

- Minimizing Distractions: A quiet zone provides a dedicated space free from noise and distractions, allowing you to focus more effectively on tasks that require concentration and attention to detail. By creating a quiet environment, you can reduce interruptions and improve your ability to stay focused and productive.

- Promoting Relaxation: A quiet zone can serve as a sanctuary where you can retreat for moments of peace and relaxation amidst the busyness of the workday. Taking short breaks in a quiet environment can help reduce stress and tension, allowing you to recharge and rejuvenate before returning to your tasks feeling refreshed and energized.

- Enhancing Creativity: Quiet environments can stimulate creativity and innovation by providing space for reflection, contemplation, and deep thinking. In a quiet zone, you can explore ideas more freely, brainstorm solutions to challenges, and engage in creative problem-solving without the distractions of noise and external stimuli.

- Supporting Mental Well-being: Excessive noise and constant stimulation can be taxing on mental health, leading to feelings of overwhelm, fatigue, and burnout. Creating a quiet zone allows you to take breaks from sensory overload and promote mental well-being by fostering a sense of calm and tranquility in your workspace.

- Improving Communication: In shared workspaces or open office environments, having designated quiet zones can facilitate better communication and collaboration by providing space for private conversations, phone calls, or focused discussions without disturbing others. This can help maintain a harmonious and respectful work environment for everyone.

Overall, establishing a quiet zone in your workspace is essential for promoting focus, relaxation, creativity, and mental well-being. Whether it's a designated corner of your office, a separate room, or noise-canceling headphones, creating a quiet environment can have significant benefits for your productivity and overall quality of work life.

The Importance of Taking Breaks at Work

Taking breaks at work is important for several reasons:

- Rest and Recovery: Breaks allow your mind and body to rest and recover from the mental and physical demands of work. Continuous periods of focused activity can lead to mental fatigue and reduced productivity. Taking breaks gives your brain and muscles a chance to relax and recharge, helping you maintain optimal performance throughout the day.

- Improved Focus and Concentration: Regular breaks can help improve your focus and concentration by preventing mental burnout and boredom. When you take breaks, you give your brain a chance to reset and refocus, making it easier to stay attentive and engaged when you return to your tasks.

- Enhanced Creativity: Breaks can stimulate creativity and problem-solving by allowing your mind to wander and make new connections. Stepping away from your work can provide fresh perspectives and insights, leading to innovative ideas and solutions.

- Reduced Stress and Anxiety: Breaks can help reduce stress and anxiety by providing opportunities for relaxation and stress relief. Taking a few minutes to practice deep breathing, stretch, or engage in a mindfulness exercise can help calm your mind and body, making you feel more refreshed and rejuvenated.

- Improved Physical Health: Taking breaks allows you to incorporate movement into your day, which is important for maintaining good physical health. Whether it's a short walk, stretching exercises, or simple desk exercises, taking breaks gives you a chance to get up and move, improving circulation, reducing muscle tension, and preventing stiffness and discomfort from prolonged sitting.

- Enhanced Well-being: Breaks contribute to overall well-being by promoting work-life balance and preventing burnout. By taking regular breaks, you can avoid overworking yourself and maintain a healthy balance between work and leisure activities, leading to greater job satisfaction and fulfillment.

Overall, taking breaks at work is essential for maintaining productivity, creativity, and well-being. Incorporating regular breaks into your work routine can help you stay focused, energized, and mentally sharp throughout the day, ultimately leading to greater success and satisfaction in your work.

How to Set Boundaries with Colleagues

Setting boundaries with colleagues is essential for maintaining a healthy and productive work environment.

The Role of Assertiveness in the Workplace

Assertiveness plays a crucial role in the workplace by facilitating effective communication, fostering respect, and promoting positive relationships among colleagues. Here are some key aspects of the role of assertiveness in the workplace:

- Expressing Needs and Preferences: Assertiveness enables individuals to express their needs, preferences, and opinions in a clear, direct, and confident manner. By communicating assertively, employees can ensure that their voice is heard and their contributions are valued in the workplace.

- Setting Boundaries: Assertiveness helps individuals set and maintain boundaries in the workplace. It allows employees to establish limits on their time, energy, and resources, and communicate these boundaries to colleagues in a respectful and assertive manner. Setting boundaries helps prevent burnout, reduce stress, and maintain a healthy work-life balance.

- Handling Conflict: Assertiveness is essential for effectively managing conflict and resolving disagreements in the workplace. Assertive communication enables individuals to address conflicts directly, express their concerns and perspectives, and work collaboratively towards finding mutually acceptable solutions. By remaining calm, confident, and respectful during conflict resolution, assertive individuals can de-escalate tense situations and promote a positive and constructive work environment.

- Negotiating and Advocating: Assertiveness is a valuable skill for negotiating and advocating for one's interests and goals in the workplace. Assertive individuals are able to assertively negotiate terms, conditions, and agreements, and advocate for themselves and their teams in discussions with colleagues, managers, and stakeholders. Assertiveness empowers employees to assert their rights, assert their ideas, and advocate for fair treatment and opportunities for themselves and their colleagues.

- Building Confidence and Self-Esteem: Assertiveness helps individuals build confidence and self-esteem in the workplace by encouraging them to assert themselves and stand up for their beliefs and values. By practicing assertive communication and behavior, employees can develop a strong sense of self-assurance, assertiveness, and self-respect, which can contribute to their success and fulfillment in their professional lives.

Overall, assertiveness plays a vital role in promoting effective communication, healthy boundaries, conflict resolution, negotiation, and self-advocacy in the workplace. By cultivating assertiveness skills, individuals can enhance their professional relationships, build confidence, and navigate the complexities of the workplace with clarity, integrity, and respect.

Effectively Communicating Your Needs

Effectively communicating your needs with colleagues is essential for fostering understanding, cooperation, and respect in the workplace. Here are some tips for effectively communicating your needs with colleagues:

- Be Clear and Specific: Clearly articulate your

needs in a concise and specific manner. Avoid vague or ambiguous language, and provide specific details to help your colleagues understand exactly what you need.

- Choose the Right Time and Place: Select an appropriate time and place to discuss your needs with your colleagues. Choose a quiet and private setting where you can have a focused conversation without interruptions.

- Use "I" Statements: Frame your communication using "I" statements to take ownership of your feelings and needs. For example, instead of saying, "You never listen to me," say, "I feel frustrated when I'm not heard during meetings."

- Express Yourself Assertively: Practice assertive communication by expressing your needs confidently and respectfully. Be firm in advocating for your needs while also being open to feedback and discussion.

- Provide Context and Explanation: Offer context or explanation for your needs to help your colleagues understand why they are important to you. Providing context can help build empathy and understanding, making it more likely that your colleagues will respect your needs.

- Listen Actively: Be attentive and receptive to your colleagues' responses and feedback. Listen actively and empathetically, and be open to their perspective and input. Avoid interrupting or dismissing their concerns, and strive to find common ground and solutions together.

- Offer Solutions or Alternatives: When communicating your needs, offer solutions or alternatives to demonstrate your willingness to collaborate and find mutually beneficial solutions. This can help alleviate any concerns or objections your colleagues may have and foster a spirit of cooperation.

- Follow Up: Follow up on your communication to ensure that your needs are being met and that any agreements or arrangements are being upheld. If necessary, schedule regular check-ins to discuss progress and address any concerns or issues that may arise.

By effectively communicating your needs with colleagues, you can promote understanding, respect, and cooperation in the workplace, leading to a more positive and productive work environment for everyone involved.

Establishing a Healthy Work-Life Balance

Work-life balance is essential for maintaining overall well-being, productivity, and satisfaction in both professional and personal life. Here's why achieving a healthy work-life balance is important, along with strategies for disconnecting after work, the importance of downtime, and techniques for avoiding burnout:

Importance of Downtime

Downtime is an important part of establishing a healthy work-life balance. Benefits include:

Rest and Recovery

- Physical Restoration: Downtime allows your body to recover from the physical strain of work. It gives your muscles a chance to relax and repair, reducing the risk of fatigue and muscle tension.

- Mental Rejuvenation: Downtime is crucial for

mental rejuvenation. It gives your brain a break from constant stimulation and cognitive tasks, allowing it to rest and restore depleted mental resources. This replenishment is essential for maintaining focus, concentration, and cognitive function over the long term.

Stress Reduction

- Psychological Relief: Downtime provides psychological relief from the pressures and demands of work. It offers a respite from deadlines, meetings, and responsibilities, allowing you to unwind and release accumulated stress.

- Emotional Well-being: Engaging in leisure activities during downtime can have a positive impact on your emotional well-being. It gives you an opportunity to indulge in activities that bring you joy and fulfillment, such as spending time with loved ones, pursuing hobbies, or enjoying nature.

Creativity and Innovation

- Unleashing Creativity: Downtime unleashes your creativity by freeing your mind from the constraints of structured work tasks. It creates space for spontaneous thoughts, imaginative ideas, and creative insights to emerge.

- Problem-Solving Skills: Downtime enhances your problem-solving skills by allowing you to approach challenges with a fresh perspective. When your mind is relaxed and unfocused, you're more likely to discover innovative solutions and overcome obstacles with ease.

Personal Growth and Reflection

- Self-Discovery: Downtime provides an opportunity for self-discovery and personal growth. It allows you to explore your interests, values, and aspirations outside of the context of work, leading to greater self-awareness and fulfillment.

- Reflection and Perspective: Downtime encourages reflection and introspection, enabling you to gain perspective on your life and career. It offers a chance to evaluate your priorities, set goals, and make decisions with clarity and intention.

Overall, downtime is essential for holistic well-being, encompassing physical, mental, emotional, and creative aspects of health. By prioritizing downtime and incorporating regular periods of rest and relaxation into your routine, you can enhance your overall quality of life, productivity, and satisfaction.

How to Disconnect After Work and Avoid Burnout

In today's interconnected world, especially with the increase in remote work, it's more important than ever to establish a healthy work-life balance. Below we will explore practical tips to help you disconnect after work and avoid burnout:

Establish a Work-Life Boundary

Set specific boundaries between work and personal time. Define designated work hours and stick to them as much as possible.

Create a ritual to mark the end of the workday, such as shutting down your computer, tidying up your workspace, or changing into comfortable clothing.

Limit Technology Use

Reduce exposure to work-related emails, messages, and notifications outside of work hours. Consider setting boundaries on when and how often you check work emails or messages.

Utilize features such as "do not disturb" mode or app blockers to minimize distractions from work-related technology during personal time.

Engage in Leisure Activities

Dedicate time to activities that you enjoy and that help you relax and unwind after work. This could include exercising, spending time outdoors, reading, listening to music, or practicing hobbies.

Schedule leisure activities into your daily or weekly routine to ensure you prioritize downtime and self-care.

Practice Mindfulness and Relaxation Techniques

Incorporate mindfulness meditation, deep breathing exercises, or progressive muscle relaxation into your daily routine to reduce stress and promote relaxation.

Take short breaks throughout the day to engage in brief mindfulness or relaxation exercises, especially during particularly busy or stressful periods.

Establish a Digital Detox Routine

Designate specific times or days when you disconnect from digital devices entirely. Use this time to engage in analog activities such as reading a book, cooking, or spending time with loved ones.

Consider implementing a "screen-free" hour before bedtime to promote better sleep quality and relaxation.

Set Realistic Expectations and Prioritize Tasks

Set realistic goals and priorities for your workday to prevent overwhelm and burnout. Focus on accomplishing the most important tasks first and avoid overcommitting yourself.

Learn to delegate tasks when necessary and communicate your workload and limitations to your supervisor or team members.

Create a Relaxing Environment

Designate a specific area in your home as a relaxation zone where you can unwind after work. Make this space comfortable and inviting with cozy furnishings, soft lighting, and soothing decor.

Consider incorporating elements such as aromatherapy, calming music, or natural elements like plants to enhance the relaxation experience.

Practice Self-Care

Prioritize self-care activities such as exercise, healthy eating, adequate sleep, and social connections. Taking care of your physical and emotional well-being is essential for preventing burnout and maintaining resilience.

Be mindful of your own needs and listen to your body's signals. If you're feeling overwhelmed or exhausted, take a step back and give yourself permission to rest and recharge.

By implementing these strategies, you can create a healthy balance between work and personal life, reduce stress, and prevent burnout, ultimately leading to greater overall well-being and job satisfaction.

In conclusion, prioritizing downtime and establishing boundaries are essential components of maintaining a healthy work-life balance and preventing burnout. By implementing the strategies discussed in this chapter, such as disconnecting after work, engaging in leisure activities, and practicing self-care, you can cultivate resilience, enhance well-being, and sustain productivity in both your professional and personal life. Remember that finding balance is an ongoing process, and it's essential to regularly reassess and adjust your approach to ensure that your needs are being met. With dedication and mindfulness, you can create a fulfilling and sustainable lifestyle that promotes overall happiness and fulfillment.

Social Interactions and Anxiety

"The strongest people are those who win battles we know nothing about."

- Unknown

In our journey to create safe spaces, we often encounter various social settings that can both enrich our lives and pose challenges to our well-being. This chapter is dedicated to navigating these social spaces with confidence and grace, ensuring that our interactions with others contribute positively to our emotional health and overall happiness.

In the pages that follow, we'll empower you with the tools and insights needed to navigate social spaces with confidence, authenticity, and self-compassion, ensuring that your interactions with others contribute positively to your overall well-being and personal growth.

Navigating Social Spaces

Navigating social situations when you're grappling with anxiety can feel like traversing a minefield, but with the right tools and mindset, you can navigate these waters with greater ease and confidence. Here's a roadmap to help you chart your course:

Techniques for Managing Anxiety in Social Settings

Navigating social situations when you're grappling with anxiety can feel like traversing a minefield, but with the right tools and mindset, you can navigate these waters with greater ease and confidence. Here's a deeper dive into some effective techniques for managing anxiety in social settings:

- Deep Breathing Exercises: Deep breathing exercises are a simple yet powerful way to calm your mind and body when faced with social anxiety. By focusing on your breath, you can ground yourself in the present moment and alleviate feelings of tension and nervousness. Try inhaling deeply through your nose, holding your breath for a few seconds, and then exhaling slowly through your mouth. Repeat this process several times until you feel more centered and calm.

- Practicing Mindfulness: Mindfulness involves paying attention to the present moment without judgment, which can be incredibly beneficial for reducing anxiety in social settings. By staying grounded in the here and now, you can prevent your mind from wandering into worrisome thoughts about future interactions or past experiences. Practice mindfulness by focusing on your senses – notice the sights, sounds, smells, and sensations around you without getting caught up in judgment or interpretation.

- Challenging Negative Thoughts: Negative thoughts are often at the root of social anxiety, fueling feelings of self-doubt and fear. Cognitive-behavioral techniques can help you challenge and reframe these negative thoughts, allowing you to approach social situations with greater confidence and clarity. When you notice yourself spiraling into a cycle of self-criticism or catastrophizing, take a moment to pause and question the validity of those thoughts. Are they based on facts, or are they distorted by anxiety? Challenge these thoughts by seeking evidence to support more realistic and balanced perspectives.

- Visualization Techniques: Visualization involves mentally rehearsing successful social interactions before they occur, which can help alleviate anxiety and boost confidence. Close your eyes and imagine yourself navigating a social situation with ease and grace. Visualize yourself engaging in conversation, making eye contact, and expressing yourself confidently. By repeatedly visualizing positive outcomes, you can reprogram your mind to expect success rather than failure in social settings.

- Progressive Muscle Relaxation: Progressive muscle relaxation is a technique that involves tensing and then releasing different muscle groups in your body to promote relaxation and reduce tension. Start by tensing your muscles tightly for a few seconds, then gradually release the tension as you exhale and relax. Move through each muscle group, from your toes to your head, taking your time to notice any areas of tension and releasing them with each breath.

Incorporating these techniques into your daily routine can help you build resilience and confidence in social situations, allowing you to navigate them with greater ease and authenticity. Remember that managing social anxiety is a journey, and it's okay to seek support from a therapist or counselor if you need additional guidance and assistance.

How to Prepare for Social Interactions

Preparing for social interactions can feel like gearing up for battle, especially when you're grappling with social anxiety. But fear not – with a little preparation and self-compassion, you can face these situations with greater confidence and ease. Here's a closer look at some strategies to help you get ready:

- Setting Realistic Expectations: Before diving into social situations, take a moment to set realistic expectations for yourself. Remind yourself that it's okay to feel nervous and that nobody expects you to be flawless. Embrace your imperfections and focus on being authentic rather than striving for perfection. Remember, it's the genuine connections that matter most.

- Practicing Self-Compassion: Be kind to yourself, my friend. Social anxiety can be tough to navigate, but that doesn't mean you're weak or inadequate. Practice self-compassion by acknowledging your fears and anxieties without judgment. Treat yourself with the same kindness and understanding you would offer to a friend in need.

- Visualizing Success: Picture this – you, confidently navigating the social scene with grace and ease. Visualize yourself engaging in conversation, making eye contact, and expressing yourself authentically. Focus on positive outcomes rather than dwelling on potential pitfalls. By envisioning success, you're priming your mind for confidence and resilience.

- Role-Playing with a Trusted Ally: Sometimes, a little rehearsal can go a long way in boosting confidence. Consider enlisting the help of a trusted friend or family member to role-play social scenarios with you. Practice engaging in conversation, handling challenging situations, and asserting yourself confidently. With each rehearsal, you'll build confidence and reduce anxiety about upcoming interactions.

- Prioritizing Self-Care: Don't forget to prioritize your well-being throughout the social whirlwind. Have a self-care plan in place for during and after social events. Whether it's taking breaks to recharge, practicing mindfulness, or scheduling downtime afterward, make sure to carve out time for yourself amidst the hustle and bustle. Your well-being matters, so don't neglect it in the midst of social obligations.

By embracing these strategies, you can approach social interactions with greater confidence, authenticity, and self-compassion. Remember, you're not alone in navigating social anxiety, and it's okay to seek support from friends, family, or a therapist if you need a helping hand along the way. You've got this!

Recognizing the Need for Alone Time

It's important to recognize and honor your need for alone time, especially when navigating social anxiety. Alone time can provide much-needed space for self-reflection, recharge, and relaxation. Pay attention to your body and mind, and don't hesitate to step away from social situations when you feel overwhelmed. Here is why alone time is so important:

- Self-Reflection: Alone time offers a precious opportunity to pause, reflect, and delve into our inner world. It allows us to reconnect with our thoughts, emotions, and aspirations without external distractions, fostering deeper self-awareness and understanding.

- Recharge and Relaxation: In the hustle and bustle of daily life, our minds and bodies often become overwhelmed by stimuli and demands. Alone time provides a much-needed break from the noise, allowing us to recharge our mental and emotional batteries and replenish our energy reserves.

- Creative Expression: Solitude nurtures creativity by providing a fertile space for ideas to blossom and imagination to flourish. It offers the freedom to explore new concepts, engage in artistic endeavors, and express ourselves authentically without inhibition.

- Stress Reduction: Spending time alone can be profoundly calming, offering a respite from the pressures and stresses of external responsibilities. It allows us to unwind, decompress, and release tension, promoting a sense of calm and tranquility.

- Personal Growth: Alone time fosters personal growth and development by encouraging introspection, self-discovery, and introspective exploration. It provides the opportunity to confront our fears, confront our shortcomings, and cultivate qualities such as resilience, self-reliance, and emotional intelligence.

- Boundaries and Self-Care: Setting aside alone time is an act of self-care and boundary-setting, affirming our commitment to prioritize our well-being and mental health. It allows us to assert our needs, establish healthy boundaries, and cultivate a greater sense of autonomy and self-respect.

Overall, alone time is not merely a luxury or indulgence but an essential aspect of our overall well-being and personal growth. By embracing solitude and carving out moments of quiet reflection, we nurture our inner world, replenish our spirit, and cultivate a deeper connection with ourselves and the world around us.

Building Supportive Relationships

Building supportive relationships is essential for our emotional well-being and overall happiness. Here's how you can cultivate meaningful connections and surround yourself with people who uplift and support you:

Choosing the Right People to Spend Time With

Choosing the right people to spend time with is like carefully selecting ingredients for a recipe; each component should complement and enhance the overall flavor of your life. Here's why the quality of your relationships matters more than the quantity:

- Alignment of Values: Surround yourself with individuals whose values align with your own. Seek out people who share similar beliefs, priorities, and goals, as they are more likely to understand and support your journey.

- Respect for Boundaries: Healthy relationships are built on mutual respect and understanding of each other's boundaries. Choose friends and companions who respect your personal space, honor your limits, and encourage open communication.

- Genuine Care and Support: Look for individuals who genuinely care about your well-being and success. True friends are there for you through thick and thin, offering a listening ear, a shoulder to lean on, and unwavering support in times of need.

- Empathy and Understanding: Surround yourself with empathetic and compassionate souls who can empathize with your experiences and emotions. Choose friends who listen without judgment, validate your feelings, and offer empathy and understanding without hesitation.

- Positive Influence: Your social circle should inspire and uplift you, motivating you to reach your full potential. Surround yourself with people who encourage growth, celebrate your achievements, and challenge you to become the best version of yourself.

- Energizing Dynamics: Pay attention to how you feel when you're around certain people. Do you feel invigorated, inspired, and alive, or do you feel drained, depleted, and emotionally exhausted? Trust your intuition and gravitate towards relationships that nourish your soul and bring joy to your heart.

Ultimately, cultivating supportive relationships is about quality over quantity. Choose friends and companions who enrich your life, uplift your spirit, and bring out the best in you. Invest your time and energy in nurturing meaningful connections that nourish your soul and foster growth, happiness, and fulfilment.

The Role of Communication in Relationships

Communication is the heartbeat of relationships, pulsating with the rhythm of connection, understanding, and intimacy. Its role is multifaceted and essential for fostering healthy and fulfilling connections between individuals. Here's how communication shapes the dynamics of relationships:

- Building Connection: Communication forms the foundation upon which relationships are built. Through verbal and nonverbal interactions, individuals establish rapport, share experiences, and cultivate a sense of connection with one another.

- Expressing Thoughts and Feelings: One of the

primary functions of communication in relationships is to express thoughts, feelings, and needs. Effective communication allows individuals to articulate their emotions, desires, and concerns, fostering understanding and empathy between partners.

- Navigating Conflict: Conflict is a natural part of any relationship, but communication serves as a tool for navigating disagreements and resolving disputes. By openly discussing conflicting viewpoints, addressing underlying issues, and seeking compromise, partners can strengthen their bond and find mutually acceptable solutions.

- Fostering Trust: Transparent and honest communication builds trust between partners, creating a safe and secure emotional environment. When individuals feel comfortable expressing themselves authentically and sharing their vulnerabilities, trust flourishes, deepening the connection between them.

- Promoting Intimacy: Communication nurtures emotional intimacy by creating opportunities for vulnerability, sharing, and mutual support.

Through deep and meaningful conversations, partners develop a deeper understanding of each other's inner worlds, strengthening their emotional bond and fostering closeness.

- Setting Boundaries: Effective communication allows individuals to set and respect boundaries within the relationship. By clearly expressing their needs, preferences, and limits, partners establish mutual understanding and create a framework for healthy interaction and respect.

- Celebrating Successes: Communication isn't just about addressing challenges; it's also about celebrating successes and joys together. By openly expressing appreciation, gratitude, and affection, partners reinforce positive behaviors and strengthen their connection.

In essence, communication serves as the lifeblood of relationships, facilitating connection, understanding, and growth. By prioritizing open, honest, and respectful communication, individuals can nurture thriving and fulfilling connections with their partners.

How to Ask for Help When Needed

Asking for help is a courageous act that reflects self-awareness and resilience. It's an acknowledgment that no one has to face life's challenges alone and that seeking support is a natural part of the human experience. Here's how to reach out for help when you need it:

- Recognize Your Needs: Start by identifying what you need assistance with, whether it's emotional support, practical help, or simply someone to listen. Take a moment to reflect on your feelings and challenges, and be honest with yourself about what kind of support would be most beneficial.

- Identify Trusted Individuals: Consider the people in your life whom you trust and feel comfortable confiding in. This could be friends, family members, mentors, or mental health professionals. Choose individuals who have demonstrated empathy, understanding, and reliability in the past.

- Open Up Honestly: When reaching out for help, it's important to be open and honest about your feelings and struggles. Share your concerns or challenges with the person you're confiding in, being as specific and transparent as possible. Expressing yourself authentically can help others understand how they can best support you.

- Be Clear About Your Needs: Clearly communicate what kind of assistance you're seeking from others. Whether you need a listening ear, practical advice, or help with a specific task, be specific about your needs and how others can best support you. Providing clarity can help ensure that you receive the help you're looking for.

- Lean on Your Support Network: Remember that you're not alone in facing life's challenges. Lean on your support network for guidance, encouragement, and assistance. True friends and loved ones will be there for you in times of need, offering a helping hand and a compassionate ear.

- Practice Self-Compassion: Finally, remember to be gentle with yourself as you navigate asking for help. Recognize that it's okay to seek support and that doing so doesn't diminish your strength or independence. Treat yourself with kindness and compassion as you reach out for the assistance you need.

By embracing vulnerability and reaching out for help when needed, you can cultivate deeper connections with others and receive the support necessary to navigate life's ups and downs with resilience and grace.

In summary, building supportive relationships requires intentional effort and communication. Choose to spend time with people who uplift and support you, communicate openly and honestly in your relationships, and don't be afraid to ask for help when needed. By cultivating strong and supportive connections, you can create a network of love, understanding, and resilience to navigate life's ups and downs.

The Power of Saying No

In the realm of safe spaces, the ability to say no is a vital tool for maintaining personal boundaries, prioritizing self-care, and fostering healthy relationships. Here's why embracing the power of no is essential within this context:

The Importance of Declining When Necessary

In any context, whether within safe spaces or beyond, the ability to decline when necessary is paramount for maintaining personal integrity, emotional well-being, and a sense of autonomy. Here's an expanded view on why this skill is particularly crucial within the framework of safe spaces:

- Honoring Personal Needs and Boundaries: Saying no allows individuals to honor their own needs, boundaries, and priorities. Within safe spaces, where the focus is on fostering an environment of respect and understanding, it's essential for individuals to recognize and uphold their personal limits. By declining requests or invitations that do not align with their values or comfort level, individuals assert their right to prioritize their well-being and protect themselves from situations that may compromise their mental health.

- Preserving Emotional Well-being: Within safe spaces, where vulnerability and authenticity are encouraged, individuals may encounter situations or interactions that trigger discomfort or distress. In such instances, the ability to decline unwanted or uncomfortable requests becomes crucial for preserving emotional well-being. Saying no allows individuals to remove themselves from situations that may cause undue stress, anxiety, or emotional harm, thereby safeguarding their mental health and promoting a sense of emotional safety within the space.

- Asserting Autonomy and Self-respect: The act of saying no is an assertion of autonomy and self-respect. It communicates that individuals have agency over their own lives and choices and refuse to be coerced or manipulated into situations that do not serve their best interests. Within safe spaces, where mutual respect and understanding are valued, the ability to decline when necessary reinforces the principle that every individual's boundaries and autonomy deserve to be respected and upheld.

- Fostering a Culture of Consent: By promoting the importance of declining when necessary within safe spaces, individuals contribute to the cultivation of a culture of consent and mutual respect. Respect for personal boundaries and autonomy forms the foundation of healthy relationships and interactions, and the practice of saying no when appropriate reinforces this principle. In doing so, individuals actively contribute to creating a space where everyone feels empowered to assert their boundaries and navigate interactions with confidence and self-assurance.

The ability to decline when necessary is essential within safe spaces as it allows individuals to honor their personal needs and boundaries, preserve their emotional well-being, assert their autonomy and self-respect, and foster a culture of consent and mutual respect. By recognizing the importance of declining unwanted or uncomfortable requests, individuals contribute to creating safe, supportive, and empowering environments where everyone's well-being is valued and respected.

How to Say No Respectfully

Declining requests or invitations can indeed be challenging, especially when done in a way that maintains respect and preserves relationships. Here's a more detailed exploration of how to say no respectfully and assertively:

- Express Appreciation: Begin by expressing genuine gratitude for the offer or opportunity extended to you. Acknowledge the thoughtfulness or kindness behind the invitation or request, even if you ultimately choose to decline. This sets a positive tone for the conversation and demonstrates that you value the relationship or gesture.

- Be Firm but Polite: When delivering your response, be firm yet polite in your communication.

Clearly and directly state your decision to decline the request, using polite language and a respectful tone. Avoid equivocating or sending mixed signals, as this may lead to misunderstandings or confusion.

- Offer a Brief Explanation (If Necessary): Depending on the nature of the request and your relationship with the individual making it, you may choose to offer a brief explanation for your decision. Keep this explanation concise and relevant, focusing on the key factors influencing your decision without delving into unnecessary detail. However, it's important to note that providing an explanation is optional, and you are not obligated to justify your choices.

- Avoid Overexplaining or Justifying: While it's natural to want to explain your decision, resist the urge to overexplain or justify yourself excessively. Remember that you have the right to prioritize your own needs and well-being, and you do not owe anyone a lengthy explanation for your choices. Keep your response concise and to the point, focusing on conveying your decision with clarity and respect.

- **Reiterate Appreciation and Maintain Respect:** Conclude your response by reiterating your appreciation for the offer or opportunity and maintaining a respectful tone throughout the interaction. Emphasize that your decision is not a reflection of any negative feelings towards the individual or their request but rather a reflection of your current priorities and boundaries.

- **Offer Alternatives (If Appropriate):** In some cases, it may be appropriate to offer alternatives or compromises that align more closely with your preferences or availability. If you genuinely wish to support the individual or contribute in some way, consider proposing alternative solutions that better suit your needs or schedule. This demonstrates your willingness to find a mutually beneficial solution while still respecting your own boundaries.

By following these guidelines, you can say no respectfully and assertively, effectively communicating your boundaries and priorities while maintaining positive relationships and mutual respect. Remember that prioritizing your own well-being is not selfish but necessary for maintaining emotional health and balance in your life.

How to Deal with the Guilt of Saying No

Navigating feelings of guilt or anxiety when saying no, particularly within the context of safe spaces, can be challenging. However, it's crucial to acknowledge that prioritizing self-care and setting boundaries is not selfish but rather essential for preserving mental and emotional well-being. Here's a deeper exploration of how to cope with the guilt of saying no:

- Practice Self-Compassion: Begin by practicing self-compassion and kindness towards yourself. Recognize that feeling guilty for saying no is a common experience and does not diminish your worth or value as a person. Offer yourself the same empathy and understanding that you would extend to a friend facing a similar situation, acknowledging that you are deserving of care and respect.

- Reframe Your Perspective: Challenge any negative beliefs or assumptions you may hold about saying no. Instead of viewing it as a rejection of others or a failure to meet their expectations, reframe it as an act of self-respect and self-care. Remind yourself that setting boundaries is an essential aspect of maintaining healthy relationships and promoting your overall well-being.

- Focus on Your Needs: Redirect your focus from feelings of guilt to a consideration of your own needs and priorities. Reflect on why you chose to say no and the positive impact it will have on your mental and emotional health. Recognize that honoring your boundaries allows you to show up as your best self in your relationships and responsibilities.

- Communicate Openly: If feelings of guilt persist, consider discussing them openly and honestly with trusted friends, family members, or a therapist. Sharing your experiences and seeking support can help validate your feelings and provide perspective on how to navigate similar situations in the future.

- Embrace Positive Outcomes: Lastly, focus on the positive outcomes of asserting your boundaries. Recognize that saying no allows you to maintain a sense of autonomy and authenticity, fostering healthier and more fulfilling relationships built on mutual respect and understanding. Celebrate your ability to advocate for yourself and prioritize your well-being, knowing that doing so ultimately benefits both you and those around you.

By practicing self-compassion, reframing your perspective, and focusing on your needs, you can effectively navigate feelings of guilt associated with saying no. Remember that setting boundaries is a necessary act of self-care and self-respect, empowering you to cultivate healthier, more fulfilling relationships and lead a more balanced and authentic life.

In navigating social spaces, we've explored invaluable strategies for managing anxiety, building supportive relationships, and asserting boundaries. From techniques to ease social anxiety to the importance of choosing the right company, and from gracefully declining unwanted requests to dealing with the guilt that may accompany it, this chapter has provided a comprehensive toolkit for navigating social interactions within safe spaces.

Remember, navigating social spaces is not about perfection but progress. Each interaction offers an opportunity for growth, self-discovery, and connection. By implementing these strategies with patience, self-compassion, and practice, you can navigate social spaces with greater ease, confidence, and authenticity. As you continue on your journey, may you find comfort in knowing that your voice, your boundaries, and your well-being are worthy of respect and protection, both within yourself and in your interactions with others.

Creating Mental and Emotional Safe Zones

"The mind is its own place, and in itself can make a heaven of hell, a hell of heaven."

- John Milton

In the tumultuous landscape of life, cultivating mental and emotional safe zones becomes essential for our well-being. These sanctuaries offer solace and refuge from the chaos, allowing us to nurture our inner selves and find peace amidst the storms. In this chapter, we'll explore various techniques and practices to create mental and emotional safe zones, empowering you to navigate life's challenges with resilience and grace.

Mental Safe Spaces

In the hustle and bustle of everyday life, finding moments of peace and tranquility within our minds can be a powerful antidote to stress and overwhelm. Here, we'll explore techniques for creating mental safe spaces that offer respite from the chaos of the external world.

Techniques for Mental Escapism

Finding moments of mental escapism is akin to hitting the refresh button for our minds. It's all about intentionally redirecting our focus away from the hustle and bustle of everyday life and immersing ourselves in activities or thoughts that bring us joy and tranquility.

One powerful avenue for mental escapism is through engaging in hobbies that ignite our passion and creativity. Whether it's painting a masterpiece, getting our hands dirty in the garden, or losing ourselves in the pages of a captivating book, these activities transport us to a realm where stress dissipates, and inspiration flourishes.

Additionally, connecting with nature can serve as a potent form of mental escapism. Stepping outside for a leisurely stroll in the park or finding a serene spot to gaze at the stars can provide a much-needed respite from the chaos of urban life. The gentle rustling of leaves, the melodious chirping of birds, or the vast expanse of the night sky—these natural wonders possess a remarkable ability to ground us and remind us of the beauty and simplicity inherent in life.

The Role of Visualization and Meditation

Visualization and meditation offer incredible avenues for nurturing our mental well-being. When we visualize, we're essentially painting pictures in our minds, creating vivid scenes that transport us to places of tranquility and calm. Picture yourself strolling along a serene beach, feeling the warmth of the sun on your skin and the gentle breeze in your hair. These mental images have a remarkable ability to soothe our minds and ease our anxieties.

Similarly, meditation acts as a balm for our busy brains. It's like hitting the pause button on the chaos of our thoughts and allowing ourselves to simply be. Through practices like focusing on our breath or repeating a calming phrase, we anchor ourselves in the present moment, letting go of the worries and stresses that weigh us down. With consistent practice, meditation becomes a sanctuary—a place where we can retreat whenever life gets overwhelming, finding peace and clarity amidst the noise.

How to Create a Mental Sanctuary During Stressful Times

Creating a mental sanctuary during stressful times is crucial for finding inner peace and stability. It's like having a secret hideaway within our minds, where we can seek solace and comfort away from the chaos of the outside world.

To craft your mental sanctuary, start by imagining a place that resonates deeply with you—a place where you feel safe, calm, and completely at ease. Whether it's a cozy cabin nestled in the woods, a serene garden bathed in sunlight, or a quiet beach at dawn, let your imagination run wild. Engage all your senses as you visualize this sanctuary, soaking in every detail—the gentle rustle of leaves, the warm embrace of sunlight, the scent of fresh flowers, and the soft touch of sand beneath your feet.

Whenever you're feeling overwhelmed or anxious, take a moment to close your eyes and retreat to your mental sanctuary. Picture yourself there, surrounded by serenity and stillness. Breathe deeply and let go of any tension or worries, allowing yourself to be fully present in this tranquil space. Remember that your mental sanctuary is always within reach, ready to offer you refuge and renewal whenever you need it.

Emotional Safety

Navigating our emotional landscape is a profound journey that requires self-awareness, compassion, and resilience. In this section, we'll explore the importance of emotional safety and delve into practical strategies for nurturing our inner well-being.

Recognizing and Validating Your Feelings

Our emotional landscape is rich and varied, like a tapestry woven from countless threads of experience. Each feeling, whether it's joy, sorrow, anger, or fear, adds depth and color to the fabric of our lives. Recognizing and validating these emotions is essential for our well-being, akin to tending to a garden where every flower has its place.

Take a moment to pause and tune in to the rhythms of your inner world. Notice the ebb and flow of emotions, like gentle waves lapping against the shore of your consciousness. Allow yourself to embrace the full spectrum of your feelings, from the brightest hues to the darkest shadows. There is no right or wrong way to feel; each emotion is valid and deserving of acknowledgment.

When faced with complex or overwhelming emotions, resist the urge to push them away or bury them beneath layers of denial. Instead, invite them in like honored guests, offering them a seat at the table of your awareness. Sit with your feelings, holding space for them with compassion and acceptance. Allow them to unfold naturally, without judgment or resistance.

In this process of recognition and validation, you honor your inner truth and affirm the legitimacy of your experiences. You create a sanctuary within yourself where every emotion is welcomed and embraced. Through this practice, you cultivate emotional safety and resilience, empowering yourself to navigate life's challenges with grace and authenticity.

Techniques for Emotional Regulation

Emotional regulation is like the captain of a ship navigating through stormy seas, steering with wisdom and skill to keep the vessel steady amidst turbulent waters. It's the art of taming the tempest within, harnessing the power of our emotions and guiding them with grace and intention.

One effective technique for emotional regulation is deep breathing, a simple yet powerful practice that anchors us in the present moment. Take slow, deliberate breaths, allowing the rhythm of your inhales and exhales to soothe your nervous system and calm the storm of emotions swirling within. With each breath, feel yourself grounding into the here and now, finding solace in the sanctuary of your own body.

Progressive muscle relaxation is another valuable tool in the toolkit of emotional regulation. By systematically tensing and releasing different muscle groups, you can release tension and stress from your body, inviting a sense of ease and tranquility to wash over you like a gentle tide. Notice the subtle shifts in sensation as you relax each muscle, savoring the sensation of release and renewal.

Mindfulness meditation offers yet another pathway to emotional regulation, inviting you to cultivate a state of open-hearted awareness and acceptance. Sit in quiet contemplation, observing the thoughts and feelings that arise within you without judgment or attachment. Like a silent witness, simply watch as the waves of emotion rise and fall, knowing that you are the vast, unchanging ocean beneath.

Incorporate these practices into your daily routine, weaving them into the fabric of your life like threads in a tapestry. As you cultivate emotional resilience and stability, you'll find yourself navigating life's challenges with greater ease and grace, anchored in the deep wellspring of peace that resides within.

How to Establish an Effective Self-Care Routine

Establishing a self-care routine is like tending to the garden of your well-being, nurturing the seeds of your soul with tender love and care. It's a vital practice that honors your holistic health and fosters resilience in the face of life's challenges. Here's why it's important and how you can begin:

Self-care is essential for maintaining balance and vitality in all aspects of your life. It encompasses activities that nourish your physical, emotional, mental, and spiritual well-being, replenishing your energy reserves and enhancing your overall quality of life. Without self-care, you risk burnout, exhaustion, and diminished resilience to stress.

The steps to establishing a self-care routine include:

- Identify Your Needs: Take time to reflect on your unique needs and preferences. What activities make you feel rejuvenated and alive? What brings you a sense of peace and fulfillment? Consider your physical, emotional, mental, and spiritual needs as you brainstorm self-care practices.

- Schedule Regular Self-Care Time: Treat self-care as a non-negotiable appointment with yourself. Block out dedicated time in your schedule for self-care activities, whether it's a daily meditation session, a weekly yoga class, or a monthly spa day.

- Choose Activities Mindfully: Select activities that resonate with you on a deep level and align with your values and interests. Whether it's journaling, painting, gardening, or hiking in nature, prioritize activities that bring you joy, relaxation, and a sense of connection to yourself.

- Practice Consistency: Consistency is key when it comes to self-care. Make a commitment to yourself to prioritize self-care regularly, even when life gets busy or stressful. Remember that self-care is not selfish but essential for your well-being and resilience.

- Adjust and Adapt: Be flexible and open to adjusting your self-care routine as needed. Life is constantly changing, and your self-care needs may evolve over time. Listen to your intuition and make modifications to your routine as necessary to ensure it continues to meet your needs effectively.

By establishing a self-care routine and prioritizing your well-being, you empower yourself to lead a more balanced, fulfilling, and resilient life. Embrace self-care as a sacred act of self-love and compassion, honoring the beautiful and intricate tapestry of your being.

Cognitive Behavioral Techniques

Navigating the labyrinth of our minds can be a daunting journey, filled with twists and turns that lead us down paths of self-doubt and negativity. Cognitive Behavioral Techniques (CBT) serve as a guiding light, illuminating the way toward greater self-awareness and mental resilience. Let's delve into the world of CBT and discover how it can empower us to challenge and transform negative thought patterns:

Quick Introduction to CBT

At its essence, Cognitive Behavioral Therapy (CBT) serves as a beacon of hope in the realm of mental health, offering a structured and evidence-based approach to understanding and overcoming our inner struggles. Developed by the pioneering psychologist Dr. Aaron Beck in the

1960s, CBT stands on the foundational principle that our thoughts, emotions, and actions are intimately interconnected, forming the intricate tapestry of our psychological landscape.

CBT operates on the premise that our perception of reality is shaped by our cognitive interpretations, and thus, altering our thoughts can lead to profound changes in our emotional experiences and behavioral patterns. This therapeutic modality guides individuals on a journey of self-discovery, illuminating the hidden corridors of their minds and uncovering the roots of their emotional distress.

Through a process of collaborative exploration and inquiry, CBT encourages individuals to identify and challenge distorted or unhelpful thoughts and beliefs known as cognitive distortions. These cognitive distortions often serve as the breeding ground for anxiety, depression, and other mental health challenges, trapping individuals in a cycle of negative thinking and self-defeating behaviors.

By shining the light of awareness on these cognitive distortions, CBT empowers individuals to question their validity and accuracy, fostering a newfound sense of cognitive flexibility and resilience. Through a series of structured exercises and interventions, individuals learn to reframe their thoughts in a more balanced and realistic manner, freeing themselves from the shackles of pessimism and self-doubt.

Ultimately, CBT is not just about understanding the intricacies of our cognitive processes; it is about harnessing the power of our minds to cultivate positive change and enhance our emotional well-being. By embracing the principles of CBT and embarking on the journey of cognitive restructuring, individuals can rewrite the narrative of their lives, paving the way for a brighter and more fulfilling future.

How to Challenge and Change Negative Thought Patterns

Cognitive restructuring, the bedrock of Cognitive Behavioral Therapy (CBT), offers a beacon of hope for those ensnared in the labyrinth of negative thought patterns. At its core, this transformative process involves shining the light of awareness on automatic negative thoughts (ANTs) and cultivating the courage to challenge their dominance over our minds.

Here are a few tips for challenging and changing your negative thought patterns:

- Awareness: Start by becoming aware of your negative thoughts. Notice when they arise and the impact they have on your mood and behavior.

- Questioning: Challenge the validity of negative thoughts by questioning their accuracy. Ask yourself if there is evidence to support these thoughts or if they are based on assumptions or interpretations.

- Reality Testing: Test the reality of your negative thoughts by considering alternative explanations or perspectives. Look for evidence that supports more balanced and realistic interpretations of the situation.

- Refocusing: Shift your focus away from negative thoughts towards more positive or neutral aspects of the situation. Redirect your attention to things you can control or solutions to the problem at hand.

- Cognitive Restructuring: Replace negative thoughts with more helpful or constructive ones. Reframe your thinking by considering alternative explanations or perspectives that are more empowering or optimistic.

- Practice Gratitude: Cultivate a habit of gratitude by focusing on the things you are thankful for. This can help counteract negative thinking patterns and foster a more positive outlook on life.

- Self-Compassion: Be kind and understanding towards yourself when challenging negative thoughts. Practice self-compassion by acknowledging that everyone experiences negative emotions and that it's okay to struggle at times.

- Seek Support: Don't hesitate to reach out to friends, family, or a mental health professional for support and guidance. Talking about your negative thoughts with others can provide valuable perspective and help you gain insight into your thinking patterns.

As you embark on this journey of cognitive exploration, remember to be gentle with yourself. Cultivate an attitude of self-compassion, recognizing that negative thoughts are not indictments of your character but simply artifacts of the human experience. With each act of cognitive reframing, you carve out a new pathway in the neural circuitry of your mind, paving the way for greater resilience and emotional well-being.

In the crucible of cognitive restructuring, every challenge becomes an opportunity for growth, every setback a stepping stone on the path to transformation. As you cultivate the habit of challenging and changing negative thought patterns, you reclaim sovereignty over your mind, unlocking the door to a future imbued with possibility and hope.

How to Incorporate CBT into Daily Life

Incorporating Cognitive Behavioral Therapy (CBT) techniques into your daily life can be immensely beneficial for improving your mental well-being. Here's how you can do it:

- Identify Negative Thought Patterns: Start by becoming more aware of your negative thought patterns throughout the day. Notice when you're experiencing thoughts that are causing distress or impacting your mood.

- Challenge Negative Thoughts: Once you've identified negative thoughts, practice challenging them using CBT techniques. Question the accuracy of these thoughts and look for evidence to support or refute them. Consider alternative explanations or perspectives that are more balanced and realistic.

- Practice Cognitive Restructuring: Actively work on replacing negative thoughts with more positive or adaptive ones. Reframe your thinking by generating alternative interpretations of situations that are less distressing or more empowering.

- Use Thought Records: Keep a thought journal or use a CBT worksheet to record and analyze your thoughts. This can help you track patterns over time and develop more effective strategies for managing them.

- Set Realistic Goals: Identify specific goals for incorporating CBT techniques into your daily routine. Start with small, achievable steps and gradually increase the complexity as you become more comfortable with the process.

- Practice Mindfulness: Incorporate mindfulness techniques into your daily life to help you stay present and aware of your thoughts and emotions. Mindfulness meditation, deep breathing exercises, and body scans can all help you cultivate greater self-awareness and emotional regulation.

- Seek Professional Guidance: Consider working with a therapist who specializes in CBT to develop a personalized treatment plan tailored to your needs. A therapist can provide guidance, support, and accountability as you work on implementing CBT techniques into your daily life.

- Be Patient and Persistent: Remember that incorporating CBT techniques into your daily life is a process that takes time and practice. Be patient with yourself and celebrate your progress along the way. Consistency and persistence are key to seeing lasting changes in your thinking and behavior.

In this chapter, we explored the creation of mental and emotional safe zones through various techniques and practices. From exploring mental escapism and the power of visualization to understanding the role of emotional regulation and cognitive restructuring, this chapter provided valuable insights into fostering inner tranquility and resilience.

By recognizing and validating our feelings, practicing emotional regulation techniques, and establishing a self-care routine, we can cultivate emotional safety and well-being. Additionally, learning about Cognitive Behavioral Therapy (CBT) introduced powerful tools for challenging negative thought patterns and promoting positive cognitive restructuring.

As we conclude this chapter, remember that creating mental and emotional safe zones is an ongoing journey that requires patience, self-compassion, and commitment. By integrating these practices into our daily lives, we can nurture our mental and emotional health and build greater resilience in the face of life's challenges.

Maintaining Your Safe Space Over Time

"A journey of a thousand miles begins with a single step."

- Lao Tzu

Safe spaces are not static entities but rather dynamic environments that evolve alongside us. In this chapter, we'll explore how safe spaces can change and grow with you, how to adapt your space to life changes, and when to create new safe spaces as needed.

The Evolving Nature of Safe Spaces

Consider how a safe space, once a cozy nook for solitary reflection, may gradually transform into a vibrant hub for social connection as our lives intersect with new relationships and communities. Or imagine how the addition of meaningful mementos, cherished artwork, or soothing colors can infuse an existing space with fresh energy and resonance, aligning it more closely with our evolving sense of self.

Moreover, our safe spaces may expand beyond the confines of physical environments to encompass virtual realms, where online communities, digital platforms, and virtual gatherings provide avenues for connection, support, and self-expression. In an ever-changing world where technology continues to blur the boundaries between physical and digital spaces, our safe spaces have the remarkable capacity to transcend traditional limitations and adapt to meet our evolving needs in both the tangible and virtual realms.

Ultimately, the beauty of safe spaces lies in their adaptability and resilience. Whether we're navigating periods of growth, transition, or uncertainty, our safe spaces stand ready to embrace us with open arms, offering comfort, support, and sanctuary every step of the way. As we continue to evolve and grow, may our safe spaces evolve alongside us, serving as steadfast companions on our journey toward wholeness and well-being.

Life is an ever-evolving journey marked by twists and turns, transitions, and transformations. As we navigate the ebb and flow of life's currents, our safe spaces serve as steadfast anchors amidst the tumultuous seas of change. However, just as life is dynamic and fluid, so too must our safe spaces be adaptable and malleable to accommodate the shifting tides of circumstance.

Whether it's a change in residence, a career transition, the arrival of a new family member, or the onset of a new chapter in life, each life change presents an opportunity to reevaluate and recalibrate our safe spaces. It's during these moments of transition that we must pause, reflect, and consider how our physical and emotional environments can best support us on our journey forward.

For instance, moving to a new home may prompt us to reimagine our safe space, infusing it with elements that reflect our evolving tastes, aspirations, and lifestyle preferences. Similarly, embarking on a new career path may inspire us to create a dedicated workspace that fosters creativity, productivity, and professional fulfillment. As we enter new phases of life, such as parenthood or retirement, our safe spaces may undergo profound transformations to accommodate the changing needs and priorities of our evolving selves.

Adapting our space to life changes requires a willingness to embrace uncertainty, flexibility, and an openness to new possibilities. It's about recognizing that change is an inherent part of the human experience and viewing it as an opportunity for growth, expansion, and renewal. By thoughtfully curating our safe spaces to align with our current realities and future aspirations, we can create sanctuaries of comfort and resilience that stand the test of time and accompany us on our journey through life's ever-changing landscapes.

When should you create a new safe space?

Life is a dynamic journey, and as we evolve and grow, so too do our needs and desires. There may come a time when the safe spaces we've cherished no longer provide the solace and comfort they once did. This isn't a failure but rather a natural progression of our journey towards self-discovery and personal growth.

Creating new safe spaces is a powerful way to honor our evolving selves and acknowledge the changes unfolding within us and around us. It's a declaration of self-love and self-care, affirming our inherent worthiness of spaces that nurture and support us in our current state of being.

The decision to create new safe spaces may arise from various circumstances. It could be prompted by a major life transition, such as moving to a new city, starting a new job, or ending a significant relationship. Alternatively, it might stem from a deep inner knowing that our existing environments no longer resonate with who we are becoming, prompting us to seek out new surroundings that align more closely with our evolving values, interests, and aspirations.

Creating new safe spaces is not just about finding physical locations; it's also about cultivating inner sanctuaries within ourselves. It's about embracing change as an opportunity for growth and transformation and recognizing that our capacity to create safe spaces is limitless.

Whether it's through redecorating a room, exploring a new hobby, or embarking on a solo adventure, the process of creating new safe spaces is a deeply personal and empowering journey. It's a reminder that we have the power to shape our environments and our experiences, and that we deserve to surround ourselves with spaces that reflect and honor the beauty of who we are, both now and in the future.

The Importance of Rituals and Routines

Rituals and routines play a crucial role in our lives, providing structure, predictability, and a sense of security. They offer a framework for consistency and stability, which can be especially comforting within safe spaces. Here's why they're important:

Establishing routines for consistency is like laying down a sturdy foundation for the structure of our daily lives. Just as a well-built foundation supports the stability of a building, routines provide structure and predictability that anchor us amidst life's uncertainties. In our safe spaces, where we seek solace and refuge from the outside world, routines serve as guiding lights, offering a familiar path to follow even in the midst of chaos.

Imagine waking up to the gentle aroma of freshly brewed coffee, wrapping your hands around a warm mug, and settling into your favorite chair to savor the first moments of the day. This simple morning ritual sets the tone for the hours ahead, infusing them with a sense of calm and purpose. Similarly, an evening routine of winding down with a good book or journaling allows us to transition from the busyness of the day to the serenity of the evening, signaling to our minds and bodies that it's time to relax and recharge.

These rituals may seem small in the grand scheme of things, but their impact is profound. They provide touchstones throughout the day, offering moments of stability and comfort that ground us in the present moment. Whether it's the reassuring rhythm of familiar activities or the soothing embrace of comforting rituals, establishing routines in our safe spaces helps us navigate life's ups and downs with grace and resilience.

Rituals play a profound role in reinforcing the sanctity of our safe spaces, infusing them with meaning and purpose that transcends the physical realm. These symbolic acts serve as anchors, tethering us to the essence of our surroundings and imbuing them with a sense of significance and belonging.

Consider the act of lighting a scented candle each evening as a signal to transition from the busyness of the day to the tranquility of the evening. This simple ritual becomes a beacon of comfort, filling the air with familiar fragrances that evoke feelings of warmth and security. With each flicker of the flame, we are reminded of the sanctuary that awaits us—a space where we can unwind, reflect, and find solace amidst life's uncertainties.

Similarly, practices such as expressing gratitude or engaging in mindfulness exercises serve to deepen our connection to our safe spaces. Whether it's taking a moment to appreciate the beauty of nature outside our window or pausing to savor a cup of tea in silence, these rituals invite us to fully inhabit the present moment and cultivate a sense of mindfulness and awareness.

By infusing our safe spaces with meaningful rituals, we not only honor their significance but also strengthen their ability to nurture and support us. These symbolic acts serve as gentle reminders of the intention and purpose behind our sanctuaries, reinforcing the idea that they are sacred spaces where we can find refuge and renewal amidst life's challenges.

As we journey through life, we undergo a constant process of growth and transformation, and our safe spaces must evolve alongside us. Adapting our routines to align with our evolving needs is essential to maintaining a sense of balance and harmony in our lives.

One way to adapt our routines is by incorporating new activities or rituals that resonate with our current circumstances and aspirations. For example, if we find ourselves seeking more moments of tranquility and reflection, we might introduce a daily meditation practice into our routine. Similarly, if our priorities shift towards fostering deeper connections with loved ones, we might schedule regular family dinners or game nights to strengthen those bonds.

Moreover, modifying existing routines to better suit our evolving lifestyle is crucial for ensuring that our safe spaces remain supportive and nurturing. This might involve adjusting the timing or duration of certain activities to accommodate changing schedules or commitments. For instance, if we find that our morning routine no longer serves us as effectively, we might experiment with different wake-up times or activities to find a better fit.

By remaining attentive to our changing needs and responsive to our inner rhythms, we can adapt our routines in ways that foster growth, resilience, and well-being. In doing so, we honor the ever-evolving nature of our selves and ensure that our safe spaces continue to serve as sanctuaries of comfort and renewal throughout life's journey.

Overcoming Challenges

In our pursuit of cultivating safe spaces, we inevitably encounter various challenges that test our resilience and adaptability. These challenges can range from external disruptions to internal struggles, each posing unique obstacles to our sense of safety and well-being. However, by acknowledging these challenges and implementing effective strategies, we can overcome them and reinforce the sanctity of our safe spaces.

Dealing with Disruptions to Your Safe Space

When disruptions infiltrate our safe spaces, they can shatter the peace and security we've worked hard to cultivate. Whether it's the incessant noise from construction work outside or the upheaval caused by a sudden life change, these external disturbances can rattle our sense of calm. In the face of such challenges, it's crucial to have coping strategies in place to reclaim the sanctuary of our safe spaces.

One approach is to establish clear boundaries to protect our space from external disruptions. This might involve setting limits on noise levels, establishing quiet hours, or creating physical barriers to block out disturbances. By asserting our boundaries, we assert our right to a peaceful environment conducive to relaxation and well-being.

Seeking support from loved ones can also provide much-needed comfort during times of upheaval. Whether it's talking through our feelings with a trusted friend or seeking practical assistance from family members, reaching out for support can help alleviate feelings of isolation and stress.

In situations where external disruptions are beyond our control, finding alternative ways to engage in self-care and relaxation becomes paramount. This might involve exploring new hobbies or activities that can be enjoyed outside of our usual safe space, such as taking a walk in nature or practicing mindfulness in a nearby park. By adapting our self-care practices to fit the circumstances, we can maintain a sense of balance and resilience even in the face of adversity.

Coping with the Absence of Physical Safe Spaces

When our physical safe spaces are out of reach—whether due to travel, moving, or unexpected circumstances—it can leave us feeling unmoored and exposed. Yet, even in the absence of familiar surroundings, we can still find solace within ourselves.

One powerful strategy is to tap into our inner resources and cultivate a sense of safety and comfort from within. Mindfulness practices, such as deep breathing or body scans, can help anchor us in the present moment and create a sense of stability amidst uncertainty. Similarly, visualization techniques allow us to mentally create and inhabit our safe spaces, even when we're physically apart from them. By conjuring up images of our favorite cozy nooks or serene landscapes, we can evoke feelings of calm and security wherever we are.

Grounding exercises, such as focusing on our senses or engaging in physical movement, can also help reconnect us with the present moment and anchor us in our surroundings. Whether it's feeling the texture of a nearby object, listening to the sounds of nature, or taking a mindful walk, these practices can help ground us and provide a sense of stability amidst the chaos.

Ultimately, coping with the absence of physical safe spaces requires us to turn inward and draw upon our inner resilience. By cultivating a sense of safety and comfort from within, we can navigate periods of transition and upheaval with grace and resilience.

Best Strategies for Internalizing Your Safe Space

Internalizing your safe space involves cultivating a sense of comfort, security, and well-being within yourself, regardless of external circumstances. Here are some strategies to help you internalize your safe space:

- Mindfulness Practices: Engage in mindfulness meditation, deep breathing exercises, or body scans to anchor yourself in the present moment and cultivate a sense of inner calm and awareness.

- Visualization Techniques: Use visualization to mentally create and inhabit your safe space. Picture yourself in a serene and comforting environment, focusing on the sights, sounds, and sensations that evoke feelings of peace and relaxation.

- Positive Affirmations: Practice affirmations to reinforce feelings of self-worth, safety, and empowerment. Repeat phrases such as "I am safe and protected" or "I trust myself to navigate challenges with grace and resilience" to cultivate a sense of inner strength and security.

- Grounding Exercises: Use grounding techniques to connect with your physical body and surroundings. Pay attention to your senses, such as feeling the ground beneath your feet, listening to the sounds around you, or noticing the details of your environment, to anchor yourself in the present moment.

- Self-Compassion Practices: Practice self-compassion by offering yourself kindness, understanding, and acceptance. Treat yourself with the same care and compassion you would extend to a loved one, especially during times of stress or difficulty.

- Emotional Regulation: Develop skills for regulating your emotions and managing stress effectively. Practice techniques such as deep breathing, progressive muscle relaxation, or journaling to process and express your feelings in healthy ways.

- Setting Boundaries: Establish clear boundaries to protect your emotional well-being and create a sense of safety within yourself. Learn to recognize and honor your limits, and assertively communicate them to others when necessary.

By incorporating these strategies into your daily life, you can cultivate a deep sense of inner peace, security, and resilience, allowing you to carry your safe space with you wherever you go.

In conclusion, the journey of creating and nurturing safe spaces is a dynamic and evolving process. As we navigate life's twists and turns, our safe spaces adapt alongside us, providing comfort, support, and sanctuary through the inevitable ups and downs. Whether we're adapting our environments to reflect life changes, establishing rituals and routines for consistency, or finding ways to internalize our safe spaces, the essence remains the same: to cultivate environments that nurture our well-being and foster a sense of belonging and security.

However, the path to maintaining safe spaces is not without its challenges. External disruptions, the absence of physical safe spaces, and the need to internalize our sense of safety all present obstacles that require resilience, adaptability, and self-compassion to overcome. By embracing these challenges as opportunities for growth and learning, we can deepen our connection to ourselves and cultivate a sense of inner peace and resilience that transcends external circumstances.

Ultimately, the journey of creating safe spaces is a deeply personal and transformative one. It's about honoring our needs, nurturing our well-being, and cultivating environments that support our growth and flourishing. As we continue on this journey, may we carry with us the wisdom and strength gained from our safe spaces, knowing that we have the power to create havens of peace and tranquility wherever life may take us.

Conclusion

As we come to the end of our exploration into safe spaces, it's a moment to pause and truly grasp the profound impact these havens can have on our lives. Throughout our journey together in this book, we've ventured into the depths of what it means to create environments that nurture our well-being and provide a sense of security and belonging.

Looking back, it's clear that safe spaces aren't just physical locations; they're sanctuaries where we find solace, comfort, and renewal amidst life's challenges. Whether it's the warmth of a cozy nook in our homes, the tranquility of nature's embrace, or the serenity of our own thoughts, these safe havens offer us the refuge and strength we need in times of need.

But our journey doesn't stop here. As we move forward, let's carry with us the insights we've gained and the wisdom we've gathered from our exploration of safe spaces. Let's continue to cultivate environments that support our growth and well-being, empowering ourselves to flourish even in the face of uncertainty and adversity.

Above all, let's remember that the power to create safe spaces lies within each of us. By honoring our needs, setting healthy boundaries, and seeking out sources of support and inspiration, we can continue to nurture spaces that nourish our souls and propel us towards self-discovery and fulfillment.

And as you step into the next chapter of your life, know that you're not alone. There's a vast network of resources and communities waiting to offer guidance, encouragement, and companionship along the way. Whether it's reaching out for therapy, finding solace in support groups, or connecting with kindred spirits, remember that seeking help is a courageous act that demonstrates our resilience and strength.

In closing, may you find solace and inspiration in the safe spaces you create, and may they serve as beacons of light and hope on your journey toward a life filled with joy, fulfillment, and authenticity.

"Peace is not the absence of chaos. It is the presence of resilience and calm within the chaos."

- Unknown

Appendix 1

In this section, you will find several worksheets and checklists to help you create a safe space. Using worksheets to help create a safe space offers several benefits:

Organization

Worksheets provide a structured format for organizing thoughts, ideas, and action steps related to creating a safe space. They help break down the process into manageable tasks, making it easier to stay organized and focused.

Clarity

Worksheets prompt individuals to consider various factors and aspects of the safe space creation process, such as lighting, privacy, and emotional needs. This encourages clarity and mindfulness in decision-making, ensuring that all relevant considerations are taken into account.

Reflection

Worksheets often include prompts for reflection, encouraging individuals to introspect and consider their emotional needs and preferences. This reflective process can lead to deeper insights and a better understanding of what elements are essential for creating a truly supportive and nurturing environment.

Actionable Steps

Worksheets typically include sections for identifying specific actions and improvements needed to transform the space into a safe and welcoming environment. This helps translate abstract ideas and intentions into concrete, actionable steps, facilitating progress and implementation.

Documentation

Worksheets serve as a written record of the safe space creation process, documenting thoughts, decisions, and progress over time. This documentation can be valuable for tracking changes, assessing effectiveness, and revisiting ideas in the future.

Overall, using worksheets can enhance the effectiveness and efficiency of the safe space creation process by providing structure, promoting clarity and reflection, facilitating action, and documenting progress. They serve as valuable tools for guiding individuals through the process of transforming a space into a sanctuary that supports their well-being and emotional needs.

Worksheet 1

Safe Space Assessment

This worksheet is designed to help you get started with creating your safe space.

Identify the Space

Describe the area you want to transform into a safe space. (e.g., bedroom, office corner, living room)

_____

Assess Current State

Lighting: Rate the current lighting in the space (poor, fair, good, excellent)

_____

Noise Level: Describe the current noise level in the space (quiet, moderate, loud)

Cleanliness: Assess the cleanliness of the space (tidy, somewhat cluttered, messy)

Privacy: Evaluate the level of privacy in the space (limited, moderate, high)

Reflect on Emotional Needs

Solitude: Consider how important solitude is for you in this space

Comfort: Reflect on what elements of comfort are necessary for you to feel at ease

Security: Identify any security measures or factors that contribute to your sense of safety

Acceptance: Reflect on the importance of feeling accepted and supported in this space

Changes and Improvements

Lighting: Note any changes needed to improve lighting (e.g., adding lamps, adjusting window treatments)

Noise Level: Identify strategies to reduce noise or create a quieter environment (e.g., soundproofing, using white noise machines)

Cleanliness: List any actions required to improve cleanliness and organization (e.g., decluttering, establishing cleaning routines)

Privacy: Note any enhancements needed to increase privacy (e.g., installing curtains, adding room dividers)

Additional Notes

Use this space to jot down any additional thoughts, ideas, or considerations for transforming the space into a safe and welcoming environment.

By completing this assessment, you can gain valuable insights into the current state of your chosen space and identify specific areas for improvement to create a safe and supportive environment that meets your emotional needs.

Worksheet 2

Safe Space Design Checklist

This checklist is designed to help you design your safe space. Space is provided to allow you to make some notes as you work on your space:

Lighting

Ensure adequate lighting sources, including both natural and artificial light, to create a warm and inviting atmosphere. Consider adjustable lighting options to accommodate different preferences and activities.

Comfortable Seating

Choose seating options that prioritize comfort and support, such as ergonomic chairs, plush cushions, or cozy armchairs. Arrange seating in a way that encourages relaxation and conversation, if applicable.

Privacy

Evaluate the level of privacy in the space and consider ways to enhance it, such as installing curtains, screens, or room dividers. Ensure that individuals feel secure and protected from external disturbances or intrusions.

Personalization

Add personal touches to the space to reflect your unique personality, preferences, and interests. Incorporate meaningful objects, such as photos, artwork, or mementos, that evoke positive emotions and memories.

Safety Measures

Conduct a safety assessment of the space to identify and address potential hazards or safety concerns. Secure loose wires, remove tripping hazards, and ensure that furniture is stable and properly positioned.

Accessibility

Ensure that the space is accessible to all individuals, including those with mobility challenges or disabilities. Provide accommodations such as ramps, handrails, or adjustable furniture to accommodate diverse needs.

Tranquil Elements

Incorporate elements that promote tranquility and relaxation, such as indoor plants, soothing colors, or calming scents. Choose decor and furnishings that contribute to a sense of serenity and well-being, avoiding clutter and overwhelming stimuli.

By using this checklist, you can ensure that your safe space is thoughtfully designed to prioritize comfort, privacy, safety, and personalization, creating a nurturing environment that supports your well-being and emotional needs.

Worksheet 3

Emotional Needs Assessment

This assessment is designed to help you determine your personal emotional needs when creating your safe space.

Reflect on Your Emotional Needs

Take a moment to reflect on your emotional needs and how they can be met in the safe space you are creating. Consider factors such as solitude, comfort, security, and acceptance. What emotions do you typically experience in this space, and what emotional support do you require?

Factors to Consider

Solitude: How important is solitude to you in this space? Do you need time alone to recharge and reflect, or do you prefer the company of others?

Comfort: What elements of comfort are essential for you to feel at ease in this space? Consider physical comfort (e.g., soft furnishings, cozy blankets) as well as emotional comfort (e.g., feeling safe and supported).

___

Security: What measures can be taken to enhance your sense of security and safety in this space? How can you create a sanctuary where you feel protected from external stressors and disturbances?

___

Acceptance: Reflect on the importance of feeling accepted and valued in this space. How can you foster an environment of acceptance and non-judgment where you can be your authentic self?

___

Identify Specific Activities or Practices to Implement

Think about specific activities or practices that help fulfill your emotional needs and promote well-being in this space. Examples may include journaling, meditation, mindfulness exercises, listening to music, practicing yoga, engaging in creative pursuits, or spending time in nature. Make a list of these activities or practices and consider how you can incorporate them into your safe space routine.

By completing this Emotional Needs Assessment, you can gain a deeper understanding of your emotional needs and preferences, allowing you to design a safe space that provides the support and comfort you require for optimal well-being and self-care.

Worksheet 4

Safe Space Maintenance Checklist

The purpose of the safe space maintenance checklist is to provide a structured approach to caring for and preserving the integrity of your safe space. By following the checklist regularly, you can ensure that your environment remains conducive to relaxation, comfort, and emotional well-being.

Regular Cleaning

Regular cleaning helps maintain cleanliness and hygiene, preventing the accumulation of dust and dirt that can detract from the space's inviting atmosphere. Take the time to establish a cleaning routine to keep your safe space tidy and inviting. Schedule tasks to maintain cleanliness:

Clutter Control

Clutter control ensures that the space remains organized and free of unnecessary items, promoting a sense of openness and tranquility. Take the time to regularly declutter surfaces and storage areas in your safe space to prevent the accumulation of unnecessary items:

Refreshment

Keep your safe space feeling fresh and welcoming by periodically updating it with new décor, scents, or furnishings. You may also consider rearranging your furniture or adding seasonal décor to breathe new life into your space.

Emotional Check-in

Regularly check in with yourself to assess whether your safe space continues to meet your emotional needs. Reflect on how you feel when you're in the space and whether any adjustments are needed to improve its supportive qualities:

Worksheet 5

Safe Space Usage Guidelines

The purpose of the Safe Space Usage Guidelines worksheet is to establish clear rules and expectations for how individuals should interact within a designated safe space.

Rules for Using the Safe Space

How Conflicts Will Be Resolved

Appendix 2

Here are some resources for further reading and support related to safe spaces, mental health, and well-being:

Books

- "The Gifts of Imperfection" by Brené Brown

- "The Body Keeps the Score: Brain, Mind, and Body in the Healing of Trauma" by Bessel van der Kolk

- "Quiet: The Power of Introverts in a World That Can't Stop Talking" by Susan Cain

- "The Highly Sensitive Person: How to Thrive When the World Overwhelms You" by Elaine N. Aron

- "The Power of Now: A Guide to Spiritual Enlightenment" by Eckhart Tolle

- "Daring Greatly: How the Courage to Be Vulnerable Transforms the Way We Live, Love, Parent, and Lead" by Brené Brown

- "Lost Connections: Why You're Depressed and How to Find Hope" by Johann Hari

- "Maybe You Should Talk to Someone: A Therapist, Her Therapist, and Our Lives Revealed" by Lori Gottlieb

- "Feeling Good: The New Mood Therapy" by David D. Burns

- "The Untethered Soul: The Journey Beyond Yourself" by Michael A. Singer

Websites

- National Alliance on Mental Illness (NAMI): Provides information, resources, and support for individuals and families affected by mental illness. Website: nami.org

- Mental Health America (MHA): Offers mental health screening tools, resources, and advocacy initiatives. Website: mentalhealthamerica.net

- Psychology Today: Features articles, blogs, and therapist directories covering various mental health topics. Website: psychologytoday.com

- Substance Abuse and Mental Health Services Administration (SAMHSA): Provides resources, treatment locators, and publications related to mental health and substance use disorders. Website: samhsa.gov

- HelpGuide: Offers articles, guides, and resources on mental health, emotional well-being, and related topics. Website: helpguide.org

- American Psychological Association (APA): Provides information on various mental health topics, research findings, and resources for finding psychologists. Website: apa.org

Online Communities

- Reddit: Subreddits like r/MentalHealth, r/Anxiety, and r/depression offer online communities where individuals can share experiences, seek advice, and offer support to others.

- 7 Cups: Provides online therapy and emotional support through trained listeners and licensed therapists. Website: 7cups.com

- Mental Health Support Community: Offers forums, chat rooms, and online support groups for individuals experiencing mental health challenges. Website: mentalhealthforum.net

- 18percent: An online peer-to-peer support community for individuals living with mental health issues. Website: 18percent.org

- Mind: Offers online support and resources for individuals experiencing mental health difficulties, including a supportive online community. Website: mind.org.uk

Podcasts

- "The Happiness Lab" by Dr. Laurie Santos: Explores the science of happiness and offers practical tips for improving mental well-being.

- "The Anxiety Coaches Podcast" by Gina Ryan: Provides insights and strategies for managing anxiety and stress in daily life.

- "Therapy Chat" by Laura Reagan, LCSW-C: Explores various aspects of mental health and wellness through interviews with therapists and experts.

- "The Science of Happiness" by Greater Good Science Center: Explores the science behind happiness and offers practical tips for cultivating a happier and more fulfilling life.

- "Therapy for Black Girls" by Dr. Joy Harden Bradford: Focuses on mental health topics relevant to Black women and offers insights and strategies for self-care and personal growth.

- "The Mental Illness Happy Hour" by Paul Gilmartin: Features candid conversations about mental health, addiction, and trauma with guests sharing their personal experiences and insights.

Apps

- Headspace: Offers guided meditation and mindfulness exercises to reduce stress, improve sleep, and boost overall well-being.

- Calm: Provides meditation sessions, sleep stories, and relaxation techniques to promote mental relaxation and mindfulness.

- Moodpath: Offers mood tracking, self-assessment, and psychoeducational content to support individuals dealing with depression and anxiety.

- Sanvello: Offers tools for stress, anxiety, and depression relief, including mood tracking, guided meditations, and cognitive behavioral therapy exercises.

- Wysa: Provides AI-driven emotional support through chat-based conversations, guided exercises, and mindfulness techniques.

- Youper: Utilizes AI to personalize therapy and coaching sessions for managing stress, anxiety, and mood disorders.

Remember to always consult with a qualified mental health professional or healthcare provider for personalized support and advice tailored to your specific needs and circumstances.

Acknowledgments

I would like to express my heartfelt gratitude to everyone who contributed to the creation of this book.

First and foremost, I extend my deepest thanks to my mentor and guide throughout this journey, [Mentor's Name]. Your wisdom, patience, and unwavering support have been invaluable, and I am profoundly grateful for your guidance every step of the way.

I am also grateful to the team at [Publisher's Name] for their dedication and expertise in bringing this project to life. From editors to designers to marketing professionals, your collaborative efforts have played a crucial role in shaping the final product.

To all the individuals who generously shared their stories, insights, and expertise for inclusion in this book, thank you. Your contributions have added depth and authenticity to the content, enriching the overall experience for readers.

A special thank you goes out to my family and friends for their unwavering support and encouragement throughout this process. Your belief in me and your willingness to lend a listening ear or a helping hand have been a source of strength and inspiration.

Last but not least, I want to express my gratitude to the readers of this book. It is my sincere hope that the words within these pages resonate with you, inspire you, and empower you to create safe spaces in your own life.

With deep appreciation,

Michelle Mann

www.ingramcontent.com/pod-product-compliance
Lightning Source LLC
LaVergne TN
LVHW021815060526
838201LV00058B/3389